Teacher Annotated Edition

THE LIVING CONSTITUTION

DENNY SCHILLINGS

GLENCOE
McGraw-Hill

New York, New York   Columbus, Ohio   Woodland Hills, California   Peoria, Illinois

About the Author

Denny L. Schillings is a social studies educator at Homewood-Flossmoor High School in the suburban Chicago community of Flossmoor, Illinois. He has taught American Government, American History, Economics, Advanced Placement European History, and World History. During his more than 30 years of experience, Mr. Schillings has been an active social studies educator. He is past-President of the National Council of the Social Studies (NCSS) and worked to develop NCSS's Curriculum Standards for Social Studies. In addition to his responsibilities at Homewood-Flossmoor High School, Mr. Schillings chaired the Social Studies Standards Committee charged with developing statewide standards of Illinois, and he remains active on various statewide assessment committees.

About the Cover

The Signing of the Constitution, painted by Helen Clark Chandler in 1940

Glencoe/McGraw-Hill

A Division of The McGraw·Hill Companies

Printed in the United States of America.

Send all inquiries to:
Glencoe/McGraw-Hill
8787 Orion Place
Columbus, OH 43240

ISBN 0-07-828064-8 (Teacher Annotated Edition)
ISBN 0-07-828063-X (Student Edition)

7 8   004   07 06 05

TABLE OF CONTENTS

★ ★ ★ ★ ★ ★ ★ ★

The following list of materials on the Constitution is a selective accumulation of materials that have been reviewed and found to be useful for students.

Baum, Lawrence. *The Supreme Court—Seventh Edition.* Washington, D.C.: Congressional Quarterly, 2000.
A superb, detailed overview of the justices, cases, and operations of the Supreme Court.

Bowen, Catherine Drinker. *Miracle at Philadelphia: The Story of the Constitutional Convention, May to September 1787.* New York: Little, Brown and Co., 1986.
Well-written narrative based on the letters and diaries of the delegates who were in Philadelphia during the summer of 1787.

Burger, Warren E. *It Is So Ordered: A Constitution Unfolds.* New York: William Morrow, 1995.
The former chief justice describes 14 cases, mostly early landmark ones such as *Marbury* v. *Madison.*

Carrel, Annette. *It's the Law! A Young Person's Guide to Our Legal System.* Volcano, CA: Volcano Press, 1994.
Overview and activities relating to kinds of law, law enforcement, the court system, and more.

Collier, Christopher and James Lincoln. *Decision in Philadelphia: The Constitutional Convention of 1787.* New York: Random House, 1986.
Narrative of the creative arguments and final product of the Constitutional Convention.

Congressional Quarterly. *American Political Leaders 1789-2000.* Washington, D.C.: Congressional Quarterly, 2000.
Biographical information on public officials, governors, and presidents, 1789-2000.

Dye, Thomas R. *Politics in States and Communities.* Upper Saddle River, NJ: Prentice Hall, 1997.
Explores the strengths of and conflicts within state and community politics.

Greenberg, Keith Elliot and Jeanne Vestal, eds. *Adolescent Rights: Are Young People Equal Under the Law?* New York: Twenty-First Century Books, 1995.
>   Provides an overview of how the legal system has treated children in the past and discusses the rights young people have today.

Harris, Laurie Lanzen, ed. *Biography for Beginners: Presidents of the United States.* Detroit, MI: Onmigraphics, Inc., 1998.
>   Presents facts and anecdotes about the personal lives, families, and duties of American presidents from George Washington through Bill Clinton.

Kronenwetter, Michael. *How Democratic Is the United States?* New York: Franklin Watts, 1994.
>   Problems of politics and government in the U.S. and ideas for change.

Lindop, Edmund. *The Changing Supreme Court.* New York: Franklin Watts, 1995.
>   Includes issues of abortion, civil rights, due process, capital punishment, and religion.

Nelson, Michael. *Guide to the Presidency.* Washington, D.C.: Congressional Quarterly, 1996.
>   This is the definitive reference work on the day-to-day operations of the presidency and the Oval Office.

Pollack, Jill S. *Women on the Hill: A History of Women in Congress.* New York: Franklin Watts, 1996.
>   Special perspective on Congress, past and present, alternating historical and biographical chapters; also contains appendices on how Congress works.

Rakove, Jack N. *Original Meanings: Politics and Ideas in the Making of the Constitution.* New York: Alfred A. Knopf, 1996.
>   Award-winning examination of the drafting of the Constitution.

Rossiter, Clinton. *1787: The Grand Convention.* New York: W.W. Norton & Company, 1987.
>   Descriptions of the individual state delegations, personalities, arguments, and concerns that shaped the Constitutional Convention.

Samuels, Cynthia K. *It's a Free Country! A Young Person's Guide to Politics and Elections.* New York: Atheneum, 1988.
>   Describes what it takes to be elected to public office. Uses case studies and numerous photographs.

★ THE MAGNA CARTA ★

(The Great Charter)

King John I was forced to sign the Magna Carta on June 15, 1215, in a field at Runneymead in southern England. The document required the king to observe the rights that the English lords understood to be theirs. Magna Carta established the idea that the king, like other English citizens, was subject to the law.

Excerpts from the Magna Carta

. . . by this our present Charter confirmed, for us and our heirs forever: that the English church shall be free, and shall have her rights entire, and liberties [whole]. . . .

. . . We also have granted to all the freemen of our kingdom, for us and for our heirs forever, all unwritten liberties . . . forever. . . .

No bailiff shall . . . put anyone to trial upon his own unsupported testimony, without reliable witnesses brought for this purpose. . . .

No freeman shall be taken or imprisoned . . . unless by the lawful judgment of his peers, or by the law of the land. . . . We will . . . not deny to any man, either justice or right.

All the aforesaid customs and liberties . . . [are] granted . . . in our kingdom . . . [and] . . . shall be observed . . . [by all].

How the Magna Carta Applies to the Constitution

In royal documents *our* is used to mean belonging to the king. Freedom for the church meant that the king would not become involved in religious matters. This is not the same as freedom of religion, since the English church at the time was Roman Catholic.

This is an early reference to the "Blessings of Liberty" in the Preamble. The idea was to give all liberties, whether specified or not, to the people and not the king.

This is an early statement of the Sixth Amendment right of the accused to be confronted by his accuser; two witnesses being required in a treason case, as in Article III, Section 3, Clause 1; and, to some extent, the Fifth Amendment right of compelling a witness.

The Constitution likewise guarantees the right to a trial in Article III, Sections 2–3 and in Amendment 6. The concept of justice is continually emphasized in the Bill of Rights.

The Preamble also establishes liberty for ". . . ourselves and our Posterity."

★ THE MAYFLOWER COMPACT ★

In November 1620, a group of religious separatists known as the Pilgrims landed off Cape Cod, in present-day Massachusetts. The group had been awarded a right to establish a plantation from the Virginia Company. However, their ship had landed much further north, and some members of the group realized that the Virginia Company had no authority to govern them. They would have to establish their own government.

To begin some form of government, the settlers agreed to cooperate under the conditions of a compact, or agreement. The Mayflower Compact was not a constitution. The Compact was less than 200 words long. It stated a theory of government, not a system of government.

The Mayflower Compact was a remarkable document. The Compact stated a revolutionary new theory about the way that people should be governed. It contained the idea that a government should be formed by the consent of the people, and that the government should work for the common good of the people. The Compact also embodied the principle that the government obtained its authority to rule from the people.

A century later, the ideas contained in the Mayflower Compact became known as the "social contract" theory of government. One hundred and fifty years later, the American colonists used the ideas of the social contract theory to justify independence from England.

The original version of the Mayflower Compact has spelling and punctuation that make it difficult to read. The spelling, punctuation, and wording in the version printed below have been modified to make the document easier to read.

In the name of God, Amen. We, whose names are signed to this document are the loyal subjects of our great leader, Lord King James. Our great king rules Great Britain, France, and Ireland. Our king rules by the grace of God, and he is the defender of the Christian faith and all things honorable.

We have undertaken a voyage on the ship *Mayflower* to plant the first colony in the Northern parts of Virginia. We have undertaken this voyage for the glory of God, the advancement of the Christian faith, and the honor of our king and country.

At this time, in the presence of God and one another, we do solemnly and mutually pledge and combine ourselves together into a single united community. We form this compact for our better ordering and preservation, and the advancement of the goals we all believe in. And in order to accomplish our ends, we will from time to time enact, make up, and frame, such just and equal laws, ordinances, acts, constitutions, and offices as shall be thought most important and convenient for the general good of the colony. In addition, we promise all due submission and obedience to the colony and its leaders.

In witness to our pledge, we have written our names on this document at Cape Cod on November 11, 1620, in the year of the rule of our leader, Lord King James of England, France, Ireland, and Scotland.

★ THE DECLARATION OF INDEPENDENCE ★

The Second Continental Congress appointed Jefferson, Adams, Franklin, Sherman, and Livingston to prepare a declaration of independence. Their task was to clarify why the colonies felt separation was the only solution to long standing problems with England. When it was signed, the Declaration of Independence did something that was perhaps even more important—it established many of the key principles for a federal system of government.

When in the Course of human events, it becomes necessary for one people to dissolve the political bands which have connected them with another, and to assume among the powers of the earth, the separate and equal station to which the Laws of Nature and of Nature's God entitle them, a decent respect to the opinions of mankind requires that they should declare the causes which impel them to the separation.

We hold these truths to be self-evident, that all men are created equal, that they are endowed by their Creator with certain unalienable Rights, that among these are Life, Liberty and the pursuit of Happiness. That to secure these rights, Governments are instituted among Men, deriving their just powers from the consent of the governed; That whenever any Form of Government becomes destructive of these ends it is the Right of the People to alter or to abolish it, and to institute new Government, laying its foundation on such principles and organizing its powers in such form, as to them shall seem most likely to effect their Safety and Happiness. Prudence, indeed, will dictate that governments long established should not be changed for light and transient causes. . . . But when a long train of abuses and usurpations, pursuing invariably the same object, evinces a design to reduce [a people] under absolute despotism, it is their right, it is their duty, to throw off such government, and to provide new guards for their future security. . . .

We, therefore, the Representatives of the United States of America, in General Congress, Assembled . . . do, in the Name, and by the Authority of the good people of these Colonies, solemnly publish and declare, That these United Colonies are, and of right ought to be Free and Independent States; . . . and that as Free and Independent States, they have full Power to levy War, conclude Peace, contract Alliances, establish Commerce, and to do all other Acts and Things which Independent States may of right do. And, for the support of this declaration with a firm reliance on the protection of Divine Providence, we mutually pledge to each other our lives, our fortunes, and our sacred honor.

★ THE ARTICLES OF CONFEDERATION ★

The Articles of Confederation represented nearly the last step in America's quest for a federal constitution. Clearly, the Articles reflected the colonial concern over liberty and mutual protection. They showed even more, however, the fear of a strong centralized government. The newly independent colonists still trusted state governments more than a national government. Article II in particular placed nearly all power into the hands of the state legislatures. This cooperative and state-based governmental style created problems for the new nation, and it was the main reason why one final step—the Constitutional Convention of 1787—was needed.

ARTICLE I. The Stile of this confederacy shall be "The United States of America."

ARTICLE II. Each state retains its sovereignty, freedom and independence, and every Power, Jurisdiction and right, which is not by this confederation expressly delegated to the United States, in Congress assembled.

ARTICLE III. The . . . states hereby . . . enter into a firm league of friendship with each other, for their common defense, the security of their Liberties, and their mutual and general welfare, binding themselves to assist each other, against all force offered to, or attacks made upon them, or any of them, on account of religion, sovereignty, trade, or any other pretence whatever.

ARTICLE IV. . . . the people of the different states in this union . . . shall be entitled to all privileges and immunities of free citizens in the several states; and the people of each state shall have free ingress and regress to and from any other state, and shall enjoy . . . all the privileges of trade and commerce, . . .

If any person guilty of, or charged with treason, felony, or other high misdemeanor in any state, shall flee from Justice, and be found in any of the United States, he shall upon demand . . . be delivered up and removed to the state having jurisdiction of his offence.

Full faith and credit shall be given in each of these states to the records, acts, and judicial proceedings of the courts and magistrates of every other state.

ARTICLE V. For the more convenient management of the general interest of the United States, delegates shall be annually appointed in such manner as the legislature of each state shall direct. . . . In determining questions in the United States, in Congress assembled, each state shall have one vote.

Freedom of speech and debate in Congress shall not be impeached or questioned in any Court. . . .

ARTICLE IX. The United States in Congress assembled, shall have the sole and exclusive right and power of determining on peace and war, . . .

ARTICLE XI. Canada acceding to this confederation, and joining in the measures of the United States, shall be admitted into and entitled to all the advantages of this union; but no other colony shall be admitted into the same unless such admission be agreed to by nine states.

ARTICLE XIII. Every state shall abide by the determinations of the United States in Congress assembled, on all questions which by this confederation are submitted to them. . . . No alteration at any time hereafter shall be made in these [Articles of this confederation] unless such alteration be agreed to in a Congress of the United States, and be afterwards confirmed by the legislatures of every state.

★ THE FEDERALIST #14 ★

In the Federalist Papers, James Madison presented arguments in favor of ratification of the new Constitution. In the excerpt below, *Federalist #14*, Madison pointed out the need for a strong central government. At the same time, he argued that the states would not lose their importance in a federal system.

"We have seen the necessity of the Union as our [strength] against foreign danger, as the conservator of peace among ourselves, as the guardian of our commerce and other common interests, as the only substitute for those military establishments which have subverted the liberties of the old world. . . .

In a democracy, the people meet and exercise the government in person; in a republic they assemble and administer it by their representatives and agents. A democracy consequently must be confined to a small spot. A republic may be extended over a large region.

The natural limit of a democracy is that distance from the central point, which will just permit the most remote citizens to assemble as often as their public functions demand, and will include no greater number than can join in those functions. The natural limit of a republic is that distance from the center which will barely allow the representatives of the people to meet as often as may be necessary for the administration of public affairs. . . . It is to be remembered that the general government is not to be charged with the whole power of making and administering the laws. Its jurisdiction is limited to certain [specific issues], which concern all the members of the republic. . . . The subordinate [states], which can extend their care to all those other objects which can be separately provided for, will retain their due authority and activity.

A second observation to be made is that the immediate object of the federal Constitution is to secure the union of the thirteen primitive States. . . . and to add to them such other states, as may arise in their neighborhoods. . . .

. . . In the third place, [the Constitution will see] that [movement] throughout the Union will be facilitated by new improvements [such as] roads . . . accommodations for travelers . . . interior navigation. . . .

A fourth and still more important consideration is . . . in regard to the safety [of the individual States. Each State should] find an inducement to make some sacrifices for the sake of the general protection. The States which lie at the greatest distance from the heart of the union, and which of course may partake least of its benefits, will be at the same time near foreign nations. These States will consequently stand on particular occasions in greatest need of the entire nation's strength and resources. It may be inconvenient for [some States] to send their representatives to the seat of government, but they would find it more so to struggle along against an invading enemy, or even to support alone the whole expense of taking precautions which may be dictated by continual danger.

. . . Happily for America, . . . [the revolutionary leaders] pursued a new and more noble course. They accomplished a revolution which has no parallel in the annals of human society. . . . If they erred most in the structure of the Union, this was the work most difficult to be executed; this is the work which has been new modeled by the act of your convention, and it is that act on which you are now to deliberate and decide."

★ ANTI-FEDERALIST CONCERNS ABOUT THE ★ CONSTITUTION

The Constitution has worked so well for so long that we sometimes forget that many patriotic Americans opposed it. Those people who opposed the Constitution were called Anti-Federalists. Some Anti-Federalists wanted only a few changes to the Constitution and some would not accept it under any conditions.

Most Anti-Federalists objected to the Constitution for a few basic reasons. At the center of their objections was the belief that the Constitution created too strong a central government. They felt that the Constitution created a single national government, not a federal government. They believed that the power of the states would be destroyed by the new Constitution. They worried that as the states lost their power to rule, a few power-hungry individuals would seize control of the government. Eventually, the Anti-Federalists argued, people would lose many of their freedoms. As one Anti-Federalist stated: "We know that private interest governs mankind generally. Power belongs originally to the people; but if rulers be not well guarded, that power may be usurped from them. People ought to be cautious in giving away power."

One of the most important persons who opposed the Constitution was Patrick Henry. Henry was not opposed to a union of the thirteen states. However, he was concerned that the proposed Constitution lacked enough protection for state and individual rights.

Henry was not alone in his desire for the protection of rights. His fears were echoed by others, including Thomas Jefferson. James Madison listened to his friends Jefferson and Henry, and soon after ratification of the Constitution, he introduced a series of amendments that created the Bill of Rights.

Patrick Henry's Objections

"A general provision should be inserted in the new system, securing to the States and the people every right which was not conceded to the general government. I trust that gentlemen . . . will see the great objects of religion, liberty of the press, trial by jury, interdiction of cruel punishments, and every other sacred right, secured, before they agree to that [Constitution].

The necessity of a bill of rights appears . . . to be greater in this government than ever it was in any government before. All nations have adopted the construction, that all rights not expressly and [definitely] reserved to the people are [inevitably] relinquished to rulers. . . . If you give up these powers, without a bill of rights, you will exhibit the most absurd thing to mankind that ever the world saw,—a government that has abandoned all its powers—the powers of direct taxation, the sword, and the purse. You have disposed of them to Congress, without a bill of rights, without check, limitation, or control."

★ RATIFICATION VOTES FOR ★ THE CONSTITUTION [1]

State	Date Ratified	Yes Votes	No Votes
Delaware	December 7, 1787	Unanimous	—
Pennsylvania	December 12, 1787	46	23
New Jersey	December 18, 1787	Unanimous	—
Georgia	January 2, 1788	Unanimous	—
Connecticut	January 9, 1788	128	40
Massachusetts	February 6, 1788	187	168
Maryland	April 26, 1788	63	11
South Carolina	May 23, 1788	149	73
New Hampshire	June 21, 1788	57	47
Virginia	June 25, 1788	89	79
New York	July 26, 1788	30	27
North Carolina	November 21, 1789	195	77
Rhode Island	May 29, 1790	34	32

[1] Saul K. Padover, and Jacob W. Landynski. *The Living U.S. Constitution.* New York: Mentor, 1983, page 26.

★ CHECKS AND BALANCES ★

To make sure that no one branch of government became too powerful, the framers gave each branch specific powers. In addition, each branch of government has some control over the actions of the other branches. The control one branch has over another is called the system of *checks and balances*. This system is illustrated in the diagram on this page.

Powers of the Legislative Branch (Congress)

Major power — *Makes the laws*

Powers over the Executive
- Can override the President's veto
- Can impeach and remove the President
- Can refuse to confirm presidential appointment
- Can refuse to ratify presidential treaties

Powers over the Judicial
- Can create lower federal courts
- Can refuse to confirm judicial appointments
- Can propose constitutional amendments
- Can impeach and remove judges

Powers of the Executive Branch (President)

Major Power — *Carries out the laws*

Powers over the Congress
- Can veto bills
- Can call special sessions of Congress
- Can recommend laws

Powers over the Judicial
- Appoints Supreme Court and federal judges
- Can grant reprieves and pardons

Powers of the Judicial Branch (Supreme Court)

Major Powers — *Interprets the laws*
— *Punishes lawbreakers*

Powers over the Congress
- Can declare laws unconstitutional

Powers over the Executive
- Can rule that laws or executive acts are unconstitutional

★ HOW A BILL BECOMES A LAW ★

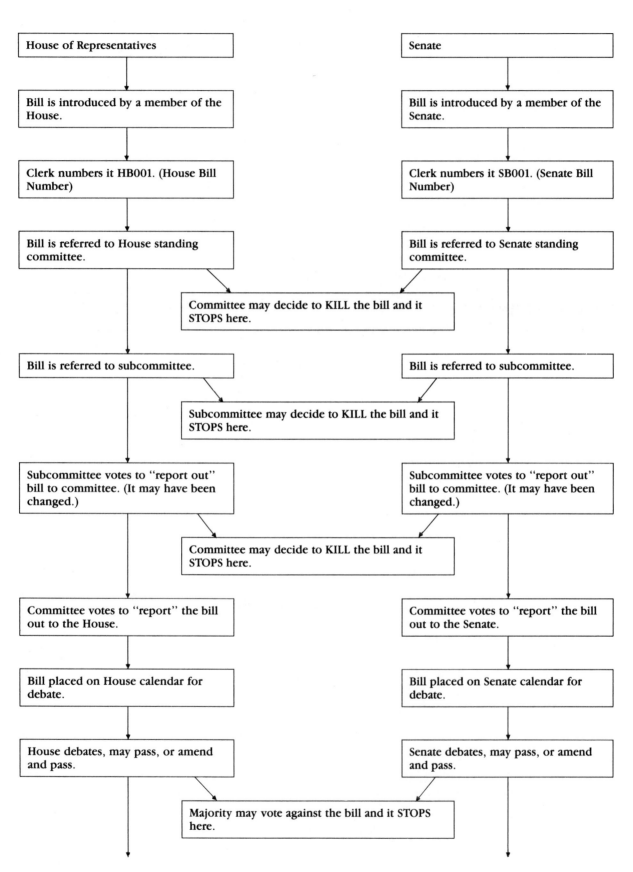

House of Representatives	Senate
Bill is introduced by a member of the House.	Bill is introduced by a member of the Senate.
Clerk numbers it HB001. (House Bill Number)	Clerk numbers it SB001. (Senate Bill Number)
Bill is referred to House standing committee.	Bill is referred to Senate standing committee.

Committee may decide to KILL the bill and it STOPS here.

Bill is referred to subcommittee.	Bill is referred to subcommittee.

Subcommittee may decide to KILL the bill and it STOPS here.

Subcommittee votes to "report out" bill to committee. (It may have been changed.)	Subcommittee votes to "report out" bill to committee. (It may have been changed.)

Committee may decide to KILL the bill and it STOPS here.

Committee votes to "report" the bill out to the House.	Committee votes to "report" the bill out to the Senate.
Bill placed on House calendar for debate.	Bill placed on Senate calendar for debate.
House debates, may pass, or amend and pass.	Senate debates, may pass, or amend and pass.

Majority may vote against the bill and it STOPS here.

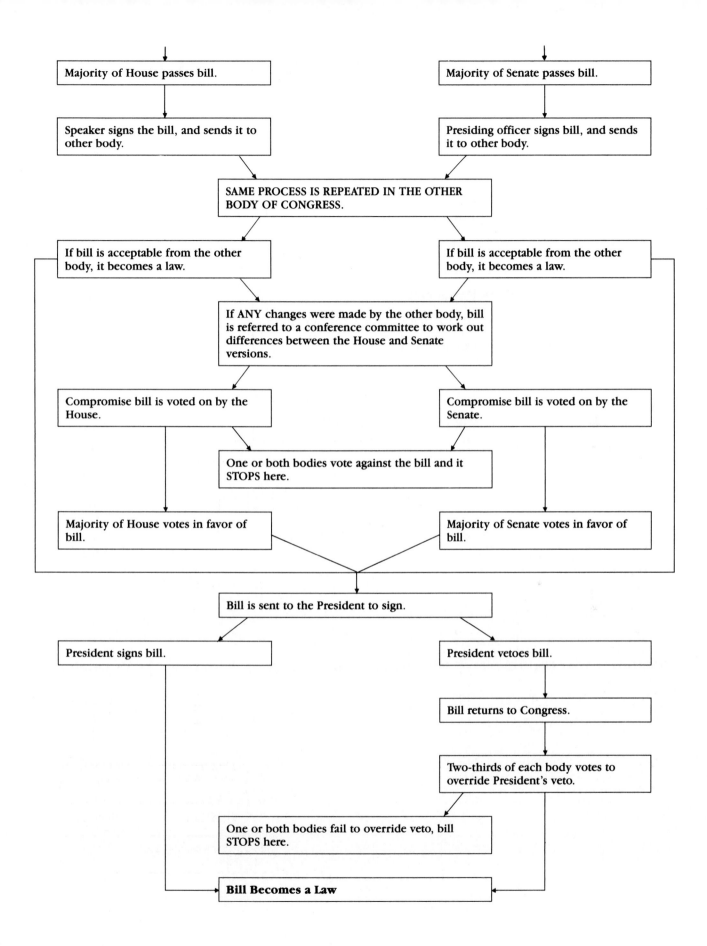

Majority of House passes bill.

Majority of Senate passes bill.

Speaker signs the bill, and sends it to other body.

Presiding officer signs bill, and sends it to other body.

SAME PROCESS IS REPEATED IN THE OTHER BODY OF CONGRESS.

If bill is acceptable from the other body, it becomes a law.

If bill is acceptable from the other body, it becomes a law.

If ANY changes were made by the other body, bill is referred to a conference committee to work out differences between the House and Senate versions.

Compromise bill is voted on by the House.

Compromise bill is voted on by the Senate.

One or both bodies vote against the bill and it STOPS here.

Majority of House votes in favor of bill.

Majority of Senate votes in favor of bill.

Bill is sent to the President to sign.

President signs bill.

President vetoes bill.

Bill returns to Congress.

Two-thirds of each body votes to override President's veto.

One or both bodies fail to override veto, bill STOPS here.

Bill Becomes a Law

★ THE EXECUTIVE BRANCH ★

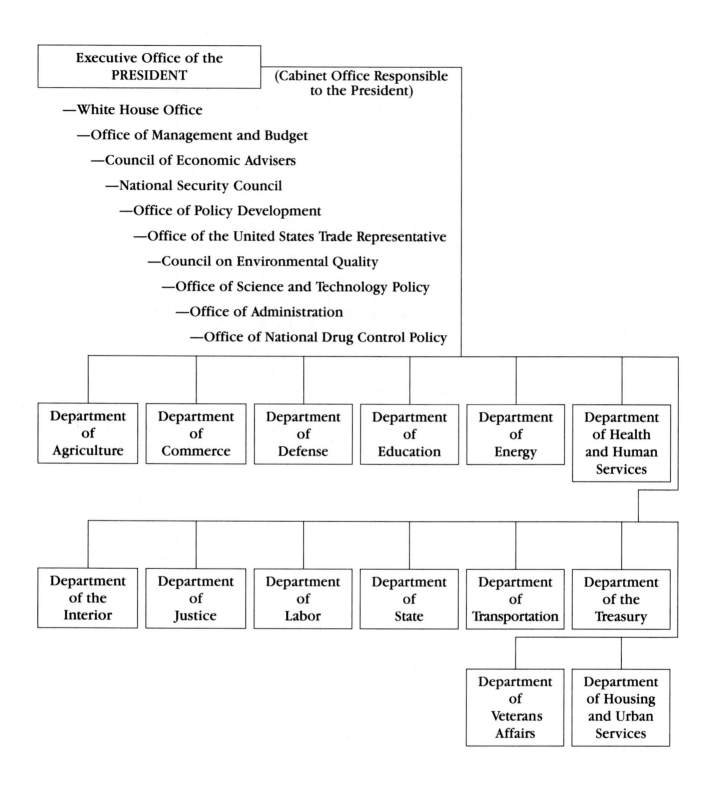

Executive Office of the
PRESIDENT

(Cabinet Office Responsible
to the President)

—White House Office

—Office of Management and Budget

—Council of Economic Advisers

—National Security Council

—Office of Policy Development

—Office of the United States Trade Representative

—Council on Environmental Quality

—Office of Science and Technology Policy

—Office of Administration

—Office of National Drug Control Policy

Department of Agriculture	Department of Commerce	Department of Defense	Department of Education	Department of Energy	Department of Health and Human Services

Department of the Interior	Department of Justice	Department of Labor	Department of State	Department of Transportation	Department of the Treasury

Department of Veterans Affairs	Department of Housing and Urban Services

★ FUNCTIONS OF THE EXECUTIVE ★ DEPARTMENTS

DEPARTMENT OF AGRICULTURE
Established - February 8, 1889
— Provides information and assistance to farmers.
— Promotes conservation and administers the Forest Service.

— Operates federal food stamp and school lunch programs.
— Tests and enforces food quality and safety.

DEPARTMENT OF COMMERCE
Established - March 4, 1913
— Conducts the census, as required by the Constitution.
— Administers the U.S. Weather Service.

— Runs the U.S. Patent Office.
— Regulates foreign and domestic commerce.

DEPARTMENT OF DEFENSE
Established - September 18, 1947
— Coordinates and manages the armed forces.

— Conducts research and engineering of military products.

DEPARTMENT OF EDUCATION
Established - September 27, 1979
— Coordinates federal aid to state and local schools.

— Promotes research to improve the quality of schools.

DEPARTMENT OF ENERGY
Established - August 4, 1977
— Administers hydroelectric and nuclear projects.
— Provides education for conserving energy.

— Promotes research on the production of energy.

DEPARTMENT OF HEALTH AND HUMAN SERVICES
Established - September 27, 1979
— Runs the social security program.
— Coordinates various health services.

— Promotes research into causes and treatments of diseases.

DEPARTMENT OF HOUSING AND URBAN DEVELOPMENT
Established - September 9, 1965
— Conducts and coordinates city planning.
— Promotes fair housing.

— Regulates and oversees various federal housing projects.

DEPARTMENT OF THE INTERIOR
Established - March 3, 1849
— Conducts mapping projects through the Geological Survey.
— Runs the national parks system.

— Provides services to Native Americans through the Bureau of Indian Affairs.

DEPARTMENT OF JUSTICE
Established - June 22, 1870
— Enforces the federal system of laws.
— Supervises the FBI and federal prison system.

— Represents the United States in legal matters.

DEPARTMENT OF LABOR
Established - March 4, 1913
— Enforces laws related to working conditions.

— Supervises various federal unemployment programs.

DEPARTMENT OF STATE
Established - September 15, 1789
— Conducts foreign affairs on behalf of the United States.
— Administers various foreign aid programs.

— Operates embassies and consulates in foreign nations.
— Issues passports.

DEPARTMENT OF TRANSPORTATION
Established - October 15, 1966
— Oversees federal funds for building and improving roads, airports, and waterways.

— Administers air safety through the Federal Aviation Agency.

DEPARTMENT OF THE TREASURY
Established - September 2, 1789
— Collects federal taxes through the Internal Revenue Service.

— Coins and prints all monies.
— Enforces customs laws.

DEPARTMENT OF VETERANS AFFAIRS
Established - March 15, 1989
— Provides medical benefits to veterans.

— Provides burial benefits for veterans.

★ PRESIDENTS OF THE UNITED STATES ★

	Years in Office	Date of Birth/Death Age When Elected	State Elected From	Occupation	Vice-President
1. George Washington	1789-1797	2/22/1732 12/14/1799 57	VA	Planter	John Adams
2. John Adams	1797-1801	10/30/1735 7/4/1826 61	MA	Lawyer	Thomas Jefferson
3. Thomas Jefferson	1801-1809	4/13/1743 7/4/1826 57	VA	Planter	Aaron Burr George Clinton
4. James Madison	1809-1817	3/16/1751 6/28/1836 57	VA	Lawyer	George Clinton Elbridge Gerry
5. James Monroe	1817-1825	4/28/1758 7/4/1831 58	VA	Lawyer	Daniel D. Tompkins
6. John Quincy Adams	1825-1829	7/11/1767 2/23/1848 57	MA	Lawyer	John C. Calhoun
7. Andrew Jackson	1829-1837	3/15/1767 6/8/1845 61	TN	Soldier	John C. Calhoun Martin Van Buren
8. Martin Van Buren	1837-1841	12/5/1782 7/24/1862 54	NY	Lawyer	Richard M. Johnson
9. William Henry Harrison [1]	1841	2/9/1773 4/4/1841 68	OH	Soldier	John Tyler
10. John Tyler	1841-1845	3/29/1790 1/18/1862 51	VA	Lawyer	NONE
11. James K. Polk	1845-1849	11/2/1795 6/15/1849 49	TN	Lawyer	George M. Dallas
12. Zachary Taylor [2]	1849-1850	11/24/1784 7/9/1850 64	LA	Soldier	Millard Fillmore
13. Millard Fillmore	1850-1853	1/7/1800 3/8/1874 50	NY	Lawyer	NONE
14. Franklin Pierce	1853-1857	11/23/1804 10/8/1869 48	NH	Lawyer	William R. King
15. James Buchanan	1857-1861	4/23/1791 6/1/1868 65	PA	Lawyer	John C. Breckinridge
16. Abraham Lincoln [3]	1861-1865	2/12/1809 4/15/1865 52	IL	Lawyer	Hannibal Hamlin Andrew Johnson
17. Andrew Johnson	1865-1869	12/29/1808 7/31/1875 56	TN	Tailor	NONE
18. Ulysses S. Grant	1869-1877	4/27/1822 7/23/1885 46	IL	Soldier	Schuyler Colfax Henry Wilson
19. Rutherford B. Hayes	1877-1881	10/4/1822 1/17/1893 54	OH	Lawyer	William A. Wheeler
20. James A. Garfield [4]	1881	11/19/1831 9/19/1881 49	OH	Teacher	Chester A. Arthur

[1] Died in Office [2] Died in Office [3] Assassinated

#	Name	Term	Birth / Death / Age	State	Occupation	Vice President
21.	Chester A. Arthur	1881-1885	10/5/1829 11/18/1886 57	NY	Lawyer	NONE
22.	Grover Cleveland	1885-1889	3/18/1837 6/24/1908 47	NY	Lawyer	Thomas A. Hendricks
23.	Benjamin Harrison	1889-1893	7/20/1833 3/13/1901 55	IN	Lawyer	Levi P. Morton
24.	Grover Cleveland	1893-1897	3/18/1837 6/24/1908 55	NY	Lawyer	Aldai E. Stevenson
25.	William McKinley [5]	1897-1901	1/29/1843 9/14/1901 54	OH	Lawyer	Garret A. Hobart Theodore Roosevelt
26.	Theodore Roosevelt	1901-1909	10/27/1858 1/6/1919 42	NY	Politician Writer	Charles W. Fairbanks
27.	William H. Taft	1909-1913	9/15/1857 3/8/1930 51	OH	Lawyer	James S. Sherman
28.	Woodrow Wilson	1913-1921	12/29/1856 2/3/1924 56	NJ	Teacher	Thomas R. Marshall
29.	Warren G. Harding [6]	1921-1923	11/2/1865 8/2/1923 55	OH	Publisher	Calvin Coolidge
30.	Calvin Coolidge	1923-1929	7/4/1872 1/5/1933 51	MA	Lawyer	Charles G. Dawes
31.	Herbert C. Hoover	1929-1933	8/10/1874 10/20/1964 54	CA	Engineer	Charles Curtis
32.	Franklin D. Roosevelt [7]	1933-1945	1/30/1882 4/12/1945 51	NY	Lawyer	John N. Garner Henry A. Wallace Harry S Truman
33.	Harry S Truman	1945-1953	5/8/1884 12/26/1972 60	MO	Haberdasher	Alben W. Barkley
34.	Dwight D. Eisenhower	1953-1961	10/14/1890 3/28/1969 62	NY PA	Soldier	Richard M. Nixon
35.	John F. Kennedy [8]	1961-1963	5/29/1917 11/22/1963 43	MA	Politician Writer	Lyndon B. Johnson
36.	Lyndon B. Johnson	1963-1969	8/27/1908 1/22/1973 55	TX	Teacher	Hubert H. Humphrey
37.	Richard M. Nixon [9]	1969-1974	1/9/1913 4/22/1994 56	NY CA	Lawyer	Spiro T. Agnew Gerald R. Ford
38.	Gerald R. Ford	1974-1977	7/14/1913 — 61	MI	Lawyer	Nelson A. Rockefeller
39.	Jimmy Carter	1977-1981	10/1/1924 — 52	GA	Businessman Farmer	Walter F. Mondale
40.	Ronald Reagan	1981-1989	2/6/1911 — 69	CA	Actor Politician	George Bush
41.	George Bush	1989-1993	6/12/1924 — 64	TX	Businessman	J. Danforth Quayle
42.	William J. Clinton	1993-2001	8/19/1946 46	AR	Politician	Albert Gore, Jr.
43.	George W. Bush	2001-	7/6/1946 — 54	TX	Businessman Politician	Richard B. Cheney

[4] Assassinated   [5] Assassinated   [6] Died in office   [7] Died in office   [8] Assassinated   [9] Resigned

★ STUDENT REVIEW OUTLINE OF THE ★ CONSTITUTION

You can use the following outline to help you find information in the Constitution or to help you prepare for a test.

PREAMBLE
States the purpose of the Constitution

ARTICLE I - THE LEGISLATIVE BRANCH
Section 1: **Congress Established**

Section 2: **House of Representatives**
Clause 1: Election and Term of Office
Clause 2: Qualifications for the House
Clause 3: Number of Representatives per State (Parts changed by Amendments 13, 14, 16)
Clause 4: Vacancies in the House
Clause 5: Officers for the House; Impeachment

Section 3: **Senate**
Clause 1: Election of Senators (Parts changed by Amendment 17)
Clause 2: Term of Office; Vacancies (Parts changed by Amendment 17)
Clause 3: Qualifications for the Senate
Clause 4: President of the Senate
Clause 5: Office for the Senate
Clause 6: Impeachment Trials
Clause 7: Impeachment Penalties

Section 4: **Congressional Elections and Meetings**
Clause 1: State Powers over Elections
Clause 2: Annual Meetings (Changed by Amendment 20)

Section 5: **Rules for Conducting Business in Congress**
Clause 1: Organization
Clause 2: Rules of Governance
Clause 3: Keeping the *Congressional Record*
Clause 4: Adjournment

Section 6: **Privileges and Restrictions of Congress**
Clause 1: Pay; Privileges
Clause 2: Restrictions on Employment of Congress

Section 7: **Passing Laws**
Clause 1: Raising Money
Clause 2: How a Bill Becomes Law
Clause 3: Presidential Veto

Section 8: **Enumerated Powers of Congress**
Clause 1: Tax; Pay Debts
Clause 2: Borrow Money
Clause 3: Regulate Trade
Clause 4: Regulate Citizenship; Bankruptcies
Clause 5: Regulate Money, Weights and Measures
Clause 6: Punish Counterfeiting
Clause 7: Establish a Postal Service
Clause 8: Issue Copyrights and Patents
Clause 9: Establish Minor Courts
Clause 10: Define and Punish Crimes on the Oceans
Clause 11: Declare War
Clause 12: Create and Support an Army
Clause 13: Create and Support a Navy
Clause 14: Make Rules for the Military
Clause 15: Utilize State Militia
Clause 16: Regulate State Militia
Clause 17: Establish the Federal Capital; Regulate Federal Lands
Clause 18: "Elastic Clause"

Section 9: **Powers Denied to the Federal Government**
Clause 1: Regulating Slave Trading (Amendment 13 made this invalid)
Clause 2: Issue of a Writ of Habeas Corpus
Clause 3: Bills of Attainder; Ex Post Facto
Clause 4: Creation of Direct Taxes
Clause 5: Taxes on Exports
Clause 6: State Commerce
Clause 7: Spending Money
Clause 8: Titles of Nobility

Section 10: **Powers Denied to the States**
Clause 1: Treaties; Coining Money; Making Laws that Violate the Federal Constitution
Clause 2: Taxes on Imports and Exports
Clause 3: Declarations of War

ARTICLE II - THE EXECUTIVE BRANCH
Section 1: **The President and Vice-President**
Clause 1: Term of Office
Clause 2: Electors

★ ★ ★ **WORKSHEET 1** ★ ★ ★

Following is a list of the dates of events that led to the development of the Constitution. Next to each date, write the event that took place on that date and briefly describe the event. (The first one is done for you.)

1. 1215: **Magna Carta is signed. The King of England is forced to sign an agreement that limits his** _____

   powers. _____

2. 1295: _____

   _____

3. 1620: _____

   _____

4. 1643: _____

   _____

5. 1689: _____

   _____

6. 1754: _____

   _____

7. 1774: _____

   _____

8. 1775: _____

   _____

9. 1776: _____

   _____

   _____

10. 1781: _____

    _____

11. 1787: _____

    _____

12. 1788: _____

    _____

13. 1791: _____

    _____

★ ★ ★ WORKSHEET 2 ★ ★ ★

When each side in a dispute gives up some of its demands in order to reach a settlement, that settlement is called a *compromise*. Many compromises were needed to create the final draft of the Constitution. Answer the following questions about the compromises made by the framers of the Constitution.

1. How did the backers of the Virginia Plan want to base representation in Congress?

   _____

   _____

2. How did small states want to base representation in Congress?

   _____

   _____

3. Describe the compromise the delegates reached concerning representation. By what name was this compromise known?

   _____

   _____

   _____

4. Name two areas, in addition to representation, where delegates reached compromises.

   _____

   _____

   _____

5. What might have been the result if delegates to the convention had not made compromises?

   _____

   _____

   _____

6. Another compromise was reached during ratification. The Federalists agreed to support a series of amendments to the Constitution. What were the amendments, and why did the Anti-Federalists think they were needed?

   _____

   _____

   _____

   _____

★ ★ ★ # WORKSHEET 3 ★ ★ ★

The following statements apply to the legislative branch as set out in Article I, Sections 1–6, of the Constitution. In the first blank under *House*, write **HR** if the statement applies to the House of Representatives, **S** if it applies to the Senate, or **B** if it applies to both. In the second blank under *Section*, write the number of the section in Article I where each statement is found.

House	Section	Statement
_____	_____	1. Must be at least twenty-five years old.
_____	_____	2. Decides on the qualifications of its members.
_____	_____	3. Must have been a citizen for at least seven years.
_____	_____	4. Cannot hold other government jobs or receive salary from other government jobs.
_____	_____	5. Cannot be arrested for civil crimes while they are meeting.
_____	_____	6. Elects its own officers.
_____	_____	7. Paid out of the Treasury of the United States.
_____	_____	8. Has the power to impeach government officials.
_____	_____	9. One-third of the entire house is elected every two years.
_____	_____	10. Must be at least thirty years old.
_____	_____	11. The Vice-President is this house's president.
_____	_____	12. Elects an official called the *president pro tempore* to run meetings.
_____	_____	13. Conducts trials of impeachment.
_____	_____	14. Must meet at least once every year.
_____	_____	15. More than half the members must be present to conduct business.
_____	_____	16. Has law-making powers.
_____	_____	17. May set its own rules of operation.
_____	_____	18. Number of members in the house is based on the state's population.
_____	_____	19. Elected for six-year terms.
_____	_____	20. Member can be punished for disorderly behavior, or even expelled.
_____	_____	21. Elected for two-year terms.
_____	_____	22. Must keep an official record of its proceedings.
_____	_____	23. Must live in the state from which they are elected.

★ ★ ★ WORKSHEET 4 ★ ★ ★

Part A.

Read the Preamble to the Constitution paying special attention to the meanings of the words. Then use a dictionary or thesaurus to write two *synonyms*—words that mean the same or nearly the same—for each word listed below.

1. perfect _____

2. union _____

3. justice _____

4. domestic _____

5. tranquility _____

6. common _____

7. defense _____

8. general _____

9. welfare _____

10. blessings _____

11. liberty _____

12. posterity _____

Part B.

Rewrite the Preamble by replacing the original wording with the synonyms you've written above. Choose your synonyms carefully to avoid changing the meaning of the Preamble.

WE THE PEOPLE of the United States, in Order to form a more

_____ _____, establish

_____, insure _____

_____, provide for the _____

_____, promote the _____

_____ and secure the _____ of _____ to ourselves and our

_____ do ordain and establish

this Constitution for the United States of America.

WORSHEET 5

Study Article I, Section 7 of the Constitution and the flowchart
"How a Bill Becomes a Law." Then answer the following questions.

1. If the President does not approve a bill, what can the Congress do to
make that bill become a law?

_____
_____
_____
_____

2. What happens to a bill when it is given to the President and the
President does not act on the bill within ten days? Include an answer
for when Congress is in session and when Congress is adjourned.

_____
_____
_____
_____

3. Most bills can originate in either house of Congress. One type of bill,
however, must begin in the House of Representatives. What type of
bill is this?

_____
_____
_____
_____

4. What happens to a bill if the House of Representatives and Senate
pass different versions of the bill?

_____
_____
_____
_____

5. Tell what must happen to a bill after it is introduced in a house of
Congress and before it is voted on by that house.

_____
_____
_____
_____

★ ★ ★ **WORKSHEET 6** ★ ★ ★

A series of statements about the powers given or denied to Congress are listed below. Part of each statement is wrong. In the space provided, write the section number and clause number where the power is found, and correct the statement. Each statement has an important word or phrase in italics to help you find the answers.

1. Congress, with the help of the President, can *regulate trade.*

   _____

2. Congress can *print money,* but cannot establish weights and measures.

   _____

3. *Copyrights* are granted by Congress for a period of twenty-five years.

   _____

4. Congress can award a famous individual a *title of nobility,* such as duke.

   _____

5. *Taxes* collected by Congress may differ from state to state.

   _____

6. *States cannot engage in war* under any circumstances.

   _____

7. The President makes the laws that punish people who *counterfeit* money.

   _____

8. The President alone can *declare war.*

   _____

9. States may *sign treaties with other countries* for purposes of trade.

   _____

10. Congressional power is limited by an *elastic clause,* that gives the President extensive powers over law making.

   _____

11. Only Congress can pass *bills of attainder.*

   _____

12. Congress can suspend the protection from a *writ of habeas corpus* at any time.

   _____

★ ★ ★ **WORKSHEET 7** ★ ★ ★

Part A.

Read Article II, Section 1, Clause 3 to learn how the President and Vice-President were originally elected. Then read Amendment 12 to learn how they are elected today. Then answer the following questions.

1. How were the President and Vice-President originally elected?

_____

_____

_____

_____

2. In your own words, explain how the President and Vice-President are now elected.

_____

_____

_____

_____

_____

3. Why do you think the method of electing the President and Vice-President was changed?

_____

_____

_____

_____

_____

Part B.

Review the qualifications for representatives and senators in Article I, and for President in Article II. Then fill in the blanks below.

	President	Senator	Representative
4. How long is the term of office?	_____	_____	_____
5. How old must they be?	_____	_____	_____
6. How long must they have been a citizen?	_____	_____	_____
7. How long must they have lived in the United States?	_____	_____	_____

★ ★ ★ **WORSHEET 8** ★ ★ ★

Below are several fictional headlines about the presidency. For each headline, write what action is referred to in the headline and tell which section and clause of Article II considers the action. The first one is done for you.

1. "Senate to Give Verdict Today on Charges Against President"
   The Senate tries cases of impeachment. Sec. 4

2. "President Orders Troops into War"

_____

_____

3. "President Moves to Have Former Aide Freed"

_____

_____

4. "President Delivers State of the Union Message to Congress"

_____

_____

5. "President Appoints Mike Binder as Under-Secretary of State"

_____

_____

6. "President to Meet with Queen on Sunday"

_____

_____

7. "President Tells Congress More Money Should Be Spent on Roads"

_____

_____

8. "President Asks Congress to Approve New Agreement with India"

_____

_____

9. "President Asks Cabinet for Ideas on Solving Budget Deficit"

_____

_____

10. "House Officially Accuses President of Wrongdoing"

_____

★ ★ ★ **WORKSHEET 9** ★ ★ ★

Complete each statement below by writing in the missing word from the word list below. All the statements concern Article III of the Constitution.

Word List

aid	compensation	inferior	treaties
appellate	confesses	jury	two
attainder	Congress	original	United States
life	Constitution	state	war
comfort	corruption	Supreme Court	witnesses

1. Federal judges are appointed for __(a)__, and from time to time receive __(b)__ for their services.

   a. _____ b. _____

2. The __(a)__ decides what punishments can be given for treason. There may not be a(n) __(b)__ of treason, however. The crime of treason cannot be held as __(c)__ of blood.

   a. _____ b. _____ c. _____

3. Treason is when someone carries out __(a)__ or gives __(b)__ and __(c)__ to enemies of the United States.

   a. _____ b. _____ c. _____

4. The Supreme Court has _____ jurisdiction in cases involving ambassadors, other public ministers, and consuls.

   _____

5. In all other cases the Supreme Court has _____ jurisdiction.

   _____

6. Anyone accused of a crime has a right to a trial by a(n) __(a)__ which is held in the __(b)__ where the crime was committed.

   a. _____ b. _____

7. Federal courts deal with all cases that involve the __(a)__, the laws of the __(b)__, and __(c)__.

   a. _____ b. _____ c. _____

8. The judicial power of the United States is vested in one __(a)__, and other __(b)__ courts.

   a. _____ b. _____

9. A person can only be found guilty of treason if __(a)__ witnesses testify, or he or she __(b)__ in open court.

   a. _____ b. _____

★ ★ ★ # WORKSHEET 10 ★ ★ ★

Use the glossary in your book or any other source to define the following terms related to the judicial branch of government.

1. Supreme Court _____

2. judicial _____
_____

3. chief justice _____
_____

4. appellate jurisdiction _____
_____

5. petit jury _____
_____

6. witness _____
_____

7. bail _____
_____

8. capital crime _____
_____

9. appeal _____
_____

10. counsel _____
_____

11. defendant _____
_____

12. grand jury _____
_____

13. indictment _____
_____

14. pardon _____
_____

15. arraignment _____

★ ★ ★ # WORKSHEET 11 ★ ★ ★

Article V shows two methods of proposing an amendment to the Constitution. Below are two lists of events that must occur for an amendment to be added, but they are not in order. Write the letter of the events on the lines below so that the events are in the correct order.

METHOD 1

A. Amendment proposed by Congress.

B. Two-thirds of state conventions ratify the amendment.

C. Two-thirds of state legislatures ratify the amendment.

D. Amendment sent to state legislatures.

E. Amendment passed by two-thirds of both houses of Congress.

F. Amendment becomes part of the Constitution.

METHOD 2

A. Two-thirds of state legislatures apply to Congress for a constitutional convention.

B. Amendment becomes part of the Constitution.

C. Congress calls a constitutional convention.

D. Two-thirds of state legislatures ratify the amendment.

E. Constitutional convention sends amendment to states.

F. Two-thirds of state legislatures ratify the amendment.

G. Constitutional convention proposes an amendment.

METHOD 1

1. _____

2. _____

3. _____

4. _____

5. _____

6. _____

METHOD 2

1. _____

2. _____

3. _____

4. _____

5. _____

6. _____

7. _____

★ ★ ★ WORKSHEET 12 ★ ★ ★

Below is an outline of Articles IV, VI, and VII of the Constitution. Fill in the missing parts of the outline using your own words. Part of the outline is done for you.

Article IV
Section 1—Official actions
   Each state will honor the official actions and records of other states. _____

Section 2—Rights of citizens
   1. Privileges

   _____

   _____

   2. Extradition
   A criminal fleeing across state lines must be returned to the state _____

   where the crime was committed. _____

   3. Return of escaped enslaved persons

   _____

   _____

Section 3—Acceptance of new states and territories
   1. Admission of new states to the union

   _____

   2. Congressional powers over federal lands

   _____

Section 4—Guarantees and protection for the states

   _____

Article VI
   1. Debts owed before the Constitution

   _____

   _____

   2. Supreme law of the United States

   _____

   _____

   3. Oaths of officials to support the Constitution

   _____

   _____

Article VII—Ratification of the Constitution

   _____

   _____

★ ★ ★ # WORKSHEET 13 ★ ★ ★

The situations below deal with violations of the Bill of Rights. For each situation, tell what the violation is, and which amendment provides protection.

1. Calvin is accused of writing several bad checks. When he appears before the judge, Calvin asks for help preparing his defense because he is too poor to afford a lawyer. The judge tells Calvin that he is sorry he is poor, but Calvin will just have to prepare his own case, without any help.

   _____

   _____

2. Marvin's boss dislikes the ideas of the Church of Every Day Salvation. Marvin tells a coworker that he belongs to the church, and soon after, Marvin's boss fires him because he belongs to the church.

   _____

   _____

3. A customer says that Betty cheated her out of $2,000 at Betty's store. The customer then sues Betty. Because Betty believes the evidence will prove her innocent, she asks the judge for a jury trial. The judge says it would be a waste of time, and that he will settle the matter himself.

   _____

   _____

   _____

4. Juanita lives near a factory that puts foul-smelling smoke in the air. Juanita and her neighbors call a meeting at Juanita's house to discuss what they can do about the smoke. However, the police block the entrance to the home and tell people that they have no right to hold a meeting.

   _____

   _____

   _____

5. Bob writes a letter to the editor complaining about the way the government is treating convicts in federal prisons. Because of this letter, Bob is arrested and placed in jail himself.

   _____

   _____

   _____

★ ★ ★ WORKSHEET 14 ★ ★ ★

The situations below deal with violations of the Bill of Rights. For each situation, tell what the violation is, and which amendment provides protection.

1. Mike is in his house watching television when two policemen knock at the door. They accuse Mike of having stolen property, enter the house, and take several things that they say do not belong to Mike. When he asks if the policemen have permission to take his things, they just laugh and leave with the property.

   _____

   _____

2. Brendan is accused of armed robbery and given a trial. The jury finds Brendan innocent. The next day the prosecutor decides that the verdict was not correct, and he orders Brendan arrested and tried for the crime again.

   _____

   _____

3. When Mary was arrested for shoplifting, she asked the judge to set bail so that she could be free while awaiting trial. The judge agreed, and set bail at one million dollars. Because Mary could not afford that amount, she remained in jail.

   _____

   _____

4. The city of Central had two newspapers. The *Central News* often printed articles in favor of the local mayor. The *Central Register,* however, was very critical of him. When the *Register* wrote that the mayor might not have the best interests of the city in mind, the mayor ordered the paper closed, and it went out of business.

   _____

   _____

5. The government lacked money to support the nation's military forces. To save money, General Pulp ordered that troops be placed in the homes of people living close to military bases. Midge lived next to an army base, and two soldiers moved into her house, even though she did not want them there.

   _____

   _____

★ ★ ★ WORKSHEET 15 ★ ★ ★

For each statement below, write a word in the blank to complete a statement that relates to Amendments 11–15. When you are finished, circle each word you have written in the word-search puzzle on the bottom of the page.

1. Federal courts do not have the _____ to try cases in which a state is sued by citizens of another state.

2. The President and Vice-President are elected by the ballots cast by citizens called _____.

3. The presidential and vice-presidential candidates who receive the _____ number of electoral votes win.

4. A vice-presidential candidate must have the same _____ as the President, because he may become President.

5. Amendments 13–15 were passed as a direct result of the _____ War.

6. The amendment, passed in 1865, abolished _____.

7. Amendment 13 allows _____ servitude only as a punishment for a crime.

8. A citizen of the United States may be born in the United States or he or she can be _____.

9. Amendment 14 says that no state can deny a person _____ process of law.

10. No state is allowed to make laws that deprive a citizen of full _____ of the law.

11. No one that has engaged in insurrection, or _____, against the United States can hold a federal office.

12. Amendment 15 says all citizens have the right to _____.

PUZZLE

```
J S D F J K L Z X C V B V E Q
U Q W E R T F O U R Y U I L U
R H J H S L P O W E R O P E A
I N V O L U N T A R Y G R C L
S F D S A A C Z X C V B O T I
D N M D V P O I I U Y T T O F
I R R U E E W Q V A S D E R I
C F G E R B H J O I K L C S C
T M N B Y V T C T X L Z T A A
I Q W E R T Y S E Y U I I O T
O A S D F R E B E L L I O N I
N A T U R A L I Z E D G N H O
R Q A S E D F R T G U H Y J N
A D U R O G R E A T E S T D S
```

★ ★ ★ **WORKSHEET 16** ★ ★ ★

Read Amendments 12–15 and answer the following questions.

1. How did the changes that Amendment 12 made change the way that the President and Vice-President were elected?

_____

_____

_____

_____

_____

_____

2. Amendment 13 abolished slavery. Why do you think it took additional amendments to give former enslaved people the same rights as other citizens?

_____

_____

_____

_____

_____

3. In your own words, describe how Amendment 14 changed the way that apportionment was set up in Article I.

_____

_____

_____

_____

_____

4. Why do you think that Amendment 15 caused a great deal of concern among political leaders in the former slave states?

_____

_____

_____

_____

_____

★ ★ ★ WORSHEET 17

WORKSHEET 17

Complete the following crossword puzzle.

ACROSS

3. Amendment 21 provides _____ of Amendment 18.

5. Amendment 17 is concerned with the election of _____.

7. He or she takes over if the President temporarily cannot fill the office.

10. A President can be elected to only _____ terms of office.

11. Amendment 19 gives women the right to _____.

13. This was made illegal in 1964. (two words)

14. He or she calls an election if a senator dies in office.

DOWN

1. He was the first Vice-President to be appointed under Amendment 25.

2. The month that congressional terms begin and end, according to Amendment 20.

4. Amendment 18 was known by this name.

6. Amendments 16–27 were all passed during this century.

8. It became legal in 1913. (two words)

9. Because of Amendment 26, an _____-year-old can now vote.

12. The District of Columbia got these with Amendment 23.

Name _____

★ ★ ★ WORKSHEET 18 ★ ★ ★

Each statement below concerns a twentieth-century amendment.
Write **T** next to the number of the statement if it is true and write **F** if it
is false. Correct the false statements on the writing lines below the
statement.

_____ 1. Congress can collect taxes on income as long as the taxes are the same
for everyone in all states.

_____

_____

_____ 2. Senators are to be elected every six years by electors chosen from their
state legislatures.

_____

_____

_____ 3. Amendment 18 prohibited the sale, importation, or export of alcoholic
beverages.

_____

_____

_____ 4. Women were given the right to vote in 1920, and the state legislatures
were given power to enforce the law.

_____

_____

_____ 5. If the President dies before taking office, the newly elected
Vice-President becomes President.

_____

_____

_____ 6. Amendment 21 repealed Amendment 18 and made alcoholic beverages
legal everywhere in the United States.

_____

_____

_____ 7. No one can be elected President more than twice.

_____

_____ 8. Citizens of the District of Columbia can vote to elect their senators and
representatives.

_____

_____

_____ 9. Poll taxes are illegal in all federal elections.

_____

_____ 10. Eighteen-year-old citizens can vote in all federal elections.

_____

Name _____

★ ★ ★ WORKSHEET 19 ★ ★ ★

    Today our government is involved in many areas of our everyday lives. Below is a list of things that the federal government regulates. In each case, briefly explain what you think the federal government does, and what part of the Constitution permits this involvement.

1. **Airline travel** _____

    _____

    _____

2. **A person's job** _____

    _____

    _____

3. **Education** _____

    _____

    _____

4. **Television and radio** _____

    _____

5. **Sports** _____

    _____

6. **Unemployed workers** _____

    _____

    _____

7. **Telephone communication** _____

    _____

    _____

8. **Microwave ovens** _____

    _____

    _____

9. **Pollution** _____

    _____

    _____

10. **Musical entertainment** _____

    _____

★ ★ ★ # WORKSHEET 20 ★ ★ ★

The Constitution gives our government the authority to act on behalf of the general welfare of its citizens. Think about things in America today that affect the welfare of people, such as the environment or unemployment. On the lines below, list five issues in which you think the government should become involved. Explain how you think the Constitution gives the federal government the authority to do each of the things you suggest.

1. _____
_____
_____
_____
_____

2. _____
_____
_____
_____
_____

3. _____
_____
_____
_____
_____

4. _____
_____
_____
_____
_____

5. _____
_____
_____
_____
_____

Name _____

★ ★ ★ CONSTITUTION TEST ★ ★ ★

Short Answer   Answer each question on the writing lines.

1. What are three qualifications to be a senator?

   _____

   _____

   _____

2. What branch of government are senators and representatives a part of?

   _____

3. Who may propose a bill in Congress?

   _____

4. What are three qualifications to be President?

   _____

   _____

   _____

5. In what two ways can an amendment to the Constitution be proposed?

   _____

   _____

6. What are three qualifications to be a representative?

   _____

   _____

   _____

7. Three-fourths of the states must approve an amendment for it to become part of the Constitution. What two assemblies can approve a constitutional amendment in a state?

   _____

   _____

8. What are the first ten amendments to the Constitution called?

   _____

9. What did Amendment 13 do?

   _____

10. What is the length of the term of office for each of the following?

    a. President _____

    b. senator _____

    c. representative _____

Multiple Choice Circle the letter of the response that best answers each question.

11. What is the *main* idea of the Preamble?
    a. to state the purpose of the Constitution
    b. to set limits on the authority of the federal government
    c. to establish the relationship of the branches of government
    d. to explain the reasoning behind the break with England

12. How is the membership of the House of Representatives determined?
    a. by the apportioned population of the states
    b. by two representatives from each state
    c. by appointment of the governor of the state according to a formula established by Congress
    d. by the state legislature of each state

13. How is representation in the Senate determined?
    a. by the apportioned population of the states
    b. by two representatives from each state
    c. by appointment of the governor of the state according to a formula established by Congress
    d. by the state legislature of each state

14. Which of the following is NOT one of the branches of government?
    a. judicial
    b. executive
    c. legislative
    d. military

15. Which governmental body has the sole right to impeach?
    a. Senate
    b. Supreme Court
    c. House of Representatives
    d. electoral college

16. Which governmental body has the sole power to try an official who is impeached?
    a. Senate
    b. Supreme Court
    c. House of Representatives
    d. electoral college

17. In what publication are the debates, laws, and other information about the activities of the legislative branch reported?
    a. the *Washington Post*
    b. the *Legislative Forum*
    c. the *Docket of the Supreme Court*
    d. the *Congressional Record*

18. What is it called when the President refuses to sign a bill into law?
    a. right of refusal
    b. legislative bargaining
    c. presidential review
    d. presidential veto

19. Which of the following is NOT an expressed power of the Congress?
    a. to tax
    b. to borrow money
    c. to coin money
    d. to declare laws unconstitutional

20. What is another term for implied powers?
    a. elastic   c. absolute
    b. expressed   d. stated

21. What officers are ALL part of the executive branch of government?
    a. President, Vice-President, and chief justice
    b. Vice-President, president pro tempore, and president of the Senate
    c. chief justice, speaker of the House, and president of the Senate
    d. cabinet officers, President, and Vice-President

22. Who elects the President?
    a. the electoral college
    b. the majority of the citizens who cast votes
    c. the legislatures of the various states
    d. the majority of the House of Representatives and Senate

23. If the President is unable to serve, the Vice-President takes his place. Who is the next federal official in line for the presidency after the Vice-President?
    a. secretary of state
    b. secretary of defense
    c. president pro tempore of the Senate
    d. speaker of the House of Representatives

24. What does Article III of the Constitution deal with?
    a. the Executive Branch
    b. the Judicial Branch
    c. the Legislative Branch
    d. the rights of an individual

25. How many justices—including the chief justice—are on the Supreme Court?
    a. Five
    b. Seven
    c. Nine
    d. Eleven

26. How long does a justice of the Supreme Court remain a member of the Court?
    a. two years
    b. four years
    c. six years
    d. for life

27. Which of the following must grant permission for a new state to enter the union?
    a. the President
    b. the Congress
    c. the Supreme Court
    d. two-thirds approval of the state legislatures

28. Which amendment guarantees freedom of religion, speech, press, assembly, and petition?
    a. First
    b. Fifth
    c. Ninth
    d. Tenth

29. In what year did the Constitution become the law of the land?
    a. 1776
    b. 1789
    c. 1791
    d. 1803

30. What is the officer called who presides over the House of Representatives?
    a. President
    b. president pro tempore
    c. speaker
    d. chairman

31. What is the officer called who presides over the Senate when the Vice-President is not in attendance?
    a. President
    b. president pro tempore
    c. speaker
    d. chairman

32. If each house of Congress has passed a different version of the same bill, where must the bill go next?
    a. the President
    b. a conference committee
    c. the Supreme Court
    d. the sub-committee where it originated

33. For what is the President responsible as commander in chief?
    a. appointing senators and representatives
    b. negotiating treaties with foreign governments
    c. administering the armed forces of the nation
    d. establishing fair interstate commerce

34. Which of the following is NOT a power of the President?

a. to declare war

b. to grant reprieves and pardons

c. to execute laws

d. to present a state of the Union address each year

35. What kind of jurisdiction does the Supreme Court have over the cases concerning ambassadors, public ministers, and disputes between states?

a. original

b. appellate

c. supervisory

d. none

Matching Write the letter of each amendment next to its description.

_____ **36.** Right of women to vote

_____ **37.** Fair bail and punishment

_____ **38.** Income tax

_____ **39.** Eighteen-year-old vote

_____ **40.** Prohibition of alcohol

_____ **41.** Free speech

_____ **42.** Restraint on congressional salaries

_____ **43.** Repeal of prohibition

_____ **44.** "Lame duck" amendment

_____ **45.** Limit on presidential terms

a. Amendment 8

b. Amendment 26

c. Amendment 19

d. Amendment 1

e. Amendment 16

f. Amendment 18

g. Amendment 27

h. Amendment 22

i. Amendment 20

j. Amendment 21

Essay Write a paragraph to answer the following question.

46. What do you think are the main reasons why the Constitution has worked so well for over two hundred years?

_____

_____

_____

_____

_____

_____

_____

_____

★ ★ ★ ANSWER KEY ★ ★ ★

Worksheet #1

1. Magna Carta is signed. The King of England is forced to sign an agreement that limits his powers.
2. Model Parliament is held. English king calls representatives together to advise him on governing England.
3. Mayflower Compact is signed. First written agreement in America concerning the making of "just and equal" laws.
4. New England Confederation is approved. English colonies agree to form a loose confederation.
5. English bill of rights is established. English king is forbidden from suspending the laws.
6. Albany Plan of Union is proposed. Benjamin Franklin suggests a plan for a federal government.
7. The First Continental Congress meets. It asks the king to give colonists direct representation in making laws.
8. The Second Continental Congress meets. It begins drafting a declaration of independence from England.
9. The Declaration of Independence is signed. It declares independence.
10. The Articles of Confederation are adopted. The states agree to cooperate with one another.
11. The Constitutional Convention meets. It produces a federal Constitution for the United States.
12. The Federalist Papers are written. They support the ratification of the Constitution. Or the Constitution is ratified.
13. The Bill of Rights is adopted. It guarantees certain individual rights.

Worksheet #2

1. The Virginia Plan called for representation based on the size of the population.
2. The small states wanted all states to have equal representation.
3. One house of the legislature would be based on population; the other, equal. It was called the Connecticut Compromise.
4. Counting of enslaved people, government control of trade
5. Answers will vary. Students may respond that the delegates would never have approved a Constitution.
6. The amendments were the Bill of Rights. The Anti-Federalists feared that a strong government would limit civil liberties and wanted guarantees written into the Constitution.

Worksheet #3

1. HR, Section 2	7. B, 6	13. S, 3	19. S, 3
2. B, 5	8. HR, 2	14. B, 4	20. B, 5
3. HR, 2	9. S, 3	15. B, 5	21. HR, 2
4. B, 6	10. S, 3	16. B, 1	22. B, 5
5. B, 6	11. S, 3	17. B, 5	23. B, 2–3
6. B, 6	12. S, 3	18. HR, 2	

Worksheet #4

1. ideal, flawless	7. security, protection
2. alliance, association	8. universal, widespread
3. fairness, legality	9. well-being, benefit
4. public, national	10. advantages, profits
5. peace, harmony	11. freedom, choice
6. collective, united	12. successors, children

Paragraph should be written so as not to change the meaning of the Preamble.

Worksheet #5

1. The Congress can pass the bill if both houses pass it by a two-thirds vote.
2. If Congress is in session, the bill becomes law. If Congress is adjourned, the bill is vetoed.
3. Bills that have to do with spending money
4. The bill must go to a conference committee where the lawmakers approve one version of the bill.
5. The bill goes to a standing committee, which must approve the bill before it can be voted on by that house.

Worksheet #6

1. Section 8, Clause 3. Congress alone regulates trade.
2. Section 8, Clause 5. Congress establishes weights and measures.
3. Section 8, Clause 8. Lifetime, plus fifty years
4. Section 9, Clause 8. Titles of nobility are not allowed.
5. Section 8, Clause 1. Must be the same
6. Section 10, Clause 3. States cannot engage in war unless invaded or in immediate danger.
7. Section 9, Clause 6. Congress cannot tax state exports.
8. Section 8, Clause 11. Only Congress can declare war.
9. Section 10, Clause 1. States cannot sign treaties.
10. Section 8, Clause 18. Clause gives Congress broad powers that are not spelled out.
11. Section 9, Clause 3. Congress cannot pass bills of attainder.
12. Section 9, Clause 2. Only in a time of crisis

Worksheet #7

1. State legislatures appoint electors equal to the number of senators and representatives. Each elector votes for two persons and the states send the votes to the Senate. The votes are counted and the person having the most votes is President and the second most votes is Vice-President. If no one has a majority, or there is a tie, the House of Representatives chooses among those who have votes.
2. Each state has electoral votes equal to the number of representatives and senators. The people in each state vote for a President and Vice-President as a team. The electors vote for the team that receives the majority of votes in that state. If no ticket receives a majority, the House decides who will be President and Vice-President.

3. Answers will vary. Students may say that the present way is more democratic, that a President and Vice-President should be members of the same party, etc.
4. Four years; six years; two years
5. Thirty-five; thirty; twenty-five
6. Must be a natural-born citizen; nine years; seven years
7. Fourteen years; does not say; does not say

Worksheet #8
1. Senate tries cases of impeachment. Section 4
2. President is commander in chief. Section 2, Clause 1
3. President can pardon offenses. Section 2, Clause 1
4. President required to report to Congress. Section 3
5. President appoints executive branch officials. Section 2, Clause 2
6. President is official host to foreign dignitaries. Section 3
7. President can recommend measures to Congress. Section 3
8. President can make treaties with consent of Congress. Section 2
9. President seeks opinions of department heads. Section 2
10. Impeachment carried out by House. Section 4

Worksheet #9
1. a. life; b. compensation
2. a. Congress; b. attainder; c. corruption
3. a. war; b. aid; c. comfort   4. original
5. appellate   6. a. jury; b. state
7. a. Constitution; b. United States; c. treaties
8. a. Supreme Court; b. inferior   9. a. two; b. confess

Worksheet #10
1. The highest federal court
2. Term used to describe the courts of law and their function
3. The head judge of the Supreme Court
4. The authority of a court to review the decisions of a lower court
5. Usually twelve citizens who make a decision in a court case
6. Someone who has seen or heard something that relates to a case in court
7. Money or other property given to the court to guarantee the appearance of an accused person in court
8. Crime in which the death penalty may be given
9. When a case is taken to a higher court for review
10. Someone that helps the accused with advice in a court case
11. A person against whom a court action is taken
12. Special jury that decides whether there is enough evidence to charge a person with a crime
13. When a grand jury formally accuses someone of committing a crime
14. When someone is officially released from punishment for a crime
15. When charges are made against a person in court

Worksheet #11
Method 1
1. A   3. D   5. B or C
2. E   4. B or C   6. F
Method 2
1. A   4. E   6. D or F
2. C   5. D or F   7. B
3. G

Worksheet #12
Article IV, Section 2, Clause 1: Citizens have the same rights in all states.
Article IV, Section 2, Clause 3: Runaway enslaved people are to be returned, but this is no longer in effect because of Amendment 13.
Article IV, Section 3, Clause 1: Congress can admit new states into the union.
Article IV, Section 3, Clause 2: Congress has control over all federal lands.
Article IV, Section 4: The United States assures the states a republican form of government.
Article IV, Article VI, Clause 1: Federal debts owed before the ratification would be honored by the U.S.
Article VI, Clause 2: The Constitution and all laws passed by Congress are more important than state or local laws.
Article VI, Clause 3: All public officials must swear to support the laws of the U.S. and the Constitution.
Article VII: When nine of the states agreed to the Constitution, it officially would go into force.

Worksheet #13
1. An accused person has the right to counsel. Amendment 6
2. Freedom of religion. Amendment 1
3. Trial by jury in civil suits. Amendment 7
4. Freedom of assembly. Amendment 1
5. Freedom of speech. Amendment 1

Worksheet #14
1. Search and seizure can only be done with a court order. Amendment 4
2. Double jeopardy is not allowed. Amendment 5
3. Excessive bail or fines cannot be imposed. Amendment 8
4. Freedom of the press. Amendment 1
5. Troops cannot be quartered in private homes. Amendment 3

Worksheet #15
1. jurisdiction   7. involuntary
2. electors   8. naturalized
3. greatest   9. due
4. qualifications   10. protection
5. Civil   11. rebellion
6. slavery   12. vote

Worksheet #16

1. A list of presidential and vice-presidential candidates is assembled. The electors vote for President from the presidential list and Vice-President from another list. The presidential candidate with the greatest number of votes wins, and the vice-presidential candidate with the greatest number of votes becomes Vice-President.
2. Former slave states were not immediately willing to give rights to freed African Americans. They claimed that the definition of citizenship was left vague by the Constitution and was one of the powers reserved to the states. Therefore, most former enslaved people were not granted many basic rights of citizens because they did not qualify as citizens.
3. The entire population of a state was to be counted for the purpose of determining seats in the House of Representatives. Prior to this, Article I had only allowed for three-fifths of all enslaved people to be counted. The net result would be an increased population for the southern states and the potential of greater voting strength in the House.
4. Many were concerned over the voting power of African Americans. They felt that African Americans would support the party of Lincoln and oppose any candidates that may have been associated with the former slave system. Since there were many former enslaved people, their vote could be the determining factor in many elections.

Worksheet #17

Across
3. repeal
5. senators
7. Vice-President
10. two

11. vote
13. poll tax
14. governor

Down
1. Ford
2. January
4. prohibition
6. twentieth

8. income tax
9. eighteen
12. electors

Worksheet #18

1. T
2. F; Senators are elected by the people of the state.
3. T
4. F; The power of enforcement was given to Congress.
5. T
6. F; Individual states could continue to prohibit alcoholic beverages.
7. T
8. F; The District of Columbia was given electors for President.
9. T
10. T

Worksheet #19

1. Answers will vary. Students might include regulating interstate commerce, setting safety standards, controlling traffic.
2. Students might include minimum wages, taxes, safety standards, unemployment insurance.
3. Students might include financial aid, research, training of teachers.
4. Students might include regulation of channels, granting of licenses, free-speech guarantees.
5. Students might include safety standards, interstate commerce, support for national teams.
6. Students might include unemployment insurance, job training, food stamps.
7. Students might include interstate commerce, regulation of standards, special systems to ensure national defense.
8. Students might include safety standards, interstate commerce, establishing standards.
9. Students might include public health measures, regulation of industry, setting standards, funding for public welfare.
10. Students might include regulation of interstate commerce, guarantees of free speech.

Worksheet #20

Answers will vary. Students might include issues such as jobs, arms control, air pollution, clean water, education, and crime. Students should cite a clause or principle from the Constitution that gives the government the authority to work in these areas.

Constitution Test

1. Must be thirty years old; must have been a citizen for at least nine years; must live in the state he or she represents.
2. Congress, or the legislative branch
3. A member of the House of Representatives or a member of the Senate
4. Must be a natural-born citizen; must be at least thirty-five years old; must have lived in the United States at least fourteen years.
5. By a two-thirds vote of both houses of Congress or by a convention called by two-thirds of the states
6. Must be at least twenty-five years old; must live in the district represented; must have lived in the U.S. for at least seven years.
7. State legislatures or special state constitutional conventions
8. Bill of Rights
9. It freed enslaved people.
10. President, four years; senator, six years; representative, two years

11. a	20. a	29. b	38. e
12. a	21. d	30. c	39. b
13. b	22. a	31. b	40. f
14. d	23. d	32. a	41. d
15. c	24. b	33. c	42. g
16. a	25. c	34. a	43. j
17. d	26. d	35. a	44. i
18. d	27. b	36. c	45. h
19. d	28. a	37. a	

46. Answers will vary. Students should mention the flexibility of the Constitution; that it can be amended; that it guarantees basic civil rights; that it provides for a strong central government and a strong executive, but has safeguards against abuses of power.

THE LIVING
CONSTITUTION

 DENNY SCHILLINGS

GLENCOE
McGraw-Hill

New York, New York   Columbus, Ohio   Woodland Hills, California   Peoria, Illinois

About the Author

Denny L. Schillings is a social studies educator at Homewood-Flossmoor High School in the suburban Chicago community of Flossmoor, Illinois. He has taught American Government, American History, Economics, Advanced Placement European History, and World History. During his more than 30 years of experience, Mr. Schillings has been an active social studies educator. He is past-President of the National Council of the Social Studies (NCSS) and worked to develop NCSS's Curriculum Standards for Social Studies. In addition to his responsibilities at Homewood-Flossmoor High School, Mr. Schillings chaired the Social Studies Standards Committee charged with developing statewide standards of Illinois, and he remains active on various statewide assessment committees.

About the Cover

The Signing of the Constitution, painted by Helen Clark Chandler in 1940

Photography Credits

Cover Robert Llewellyn; **2** The Historical Society of PA; **4** file photo **6** Thomas Gilcrease Institute of American History and Art; **8** Robert Llewellyn; **11** Brad Markel/Gamma Liaison; **13** AP/Wide World Photos; **14** "Harper's Weekly," March 28, 1868; **16** Andrew Popper/Picture Group; **20** David Hume Kennerly/TIME Magazine; **23** S. Tretick/Sygma; **26** Everett C. Johnson; **28** J.P. Laffont/Sygma. **30** Brad Markel/Gamma Liaison; **32** Supreme Court Historical Society; **37** courtesy the Levi Coffin House Association; **39** (l) Stock Montage Inc., (r) Brad Markel/Gamma Liaison; **40** Frank Johnston/Black Star; **41** Brent Jones; **44** Comstock Stock Photography; **46** Bob Daemmrich; **50** Michael Sullivan/TexaStock; **53** Fred Ward/Black Star; **54** David E. Kennedy/TexaStock; **56** Culver Pictures; **59 61** AP/Wide World Photos; **62** Supreme Court Historical Society; **65** Brad Bower/Picture Group; **67** Antonio Suarez/TIME Magazine; **68** AP/Wide World Photos.

Glencoe/McGraw-Hill

A Division of The **McGraw·Hill** *Companies*

Printed in the United States of America.

Send all inquiries to:
Glencoe/McGraw-Hill
8787 Orion Place
Columbus, OH 43240

ISBN 0-07-828063-X (Student Edition)

3 4 5 6   004   06 05 04 03

TABLE OF CONTENTS

★　★　★　★　★　★　★　★

The Story of the Constitution

The United States Constitution is a remarkable document. No other document in history has been so effective at doing what it was created to do. The framers of the Constitution were a brilliant group of men who based much of their work on ideas that were many centuries old.

The English Background

The roots of our system of government, with citizens selecting leaders and making their own laws, can be traced to Ancient Greece. Although the Constitution's framers made use of Greek examples, they most often looked to England as the source of their ideas. By the mid-1100s, Englishmen were living under a single ruler and a system of law known as **common law.** Common law had been developing for centuries and was not written down. Instead it was simply *understood* by the people.

In 1215, a group of nobles forced the English king to sign a charter limiting his powers. This charter, known as the **Magna Carta,** gave birth to the idea of civil liberties on which our Constitution is based.

In the late 1200s, the first **Model Parliament** was summoned by the king. This partly elected body gave Englishmen a greater say in how they were ruled. It was an early form of **representative government.**

By the late 1600s, civil war and revolution had weakened the power of the king. In 1689, parliament used its authority to pass a **Bill of Rights.** This bill limited the king's power to suspend laws and defined the rights of citizens. It eventually served as a model for the Constitution's framers.

English Ideas Move to North America

With the exploration and settlement of North America, English ideas of government moved across the sea. In 1620, the founders of Plymouth colony drafted the first charter of self-government in the New World, an agreement known as the **Mayflower Compact.**

The new colonies were often a testing ground for experiments in cooperative government. In the mid-1600s, several New England colonies banded together to form a **confederation,** a loose union without a strong central government. The **United Colonies of New England** was pledged to friendship and mutual aid, but gradually fell apart for lack of either.

Timeline for Lesson 1

The following events and documents were important to the development of the United States Constitution.

COMMON LAW DEVELOPS IN ENGLAND — circa 1150
These laws became the basis for fair and constant interpretation of the law in constitutional systems.

MAGNA CARTA SIGNED — 1215
King of England forced to sign an agreement limiting his powers.

MODEL PARLIAMENT HELD — 1295
English king called representatives together to advise him on governing England. This became the basis for representative government.

OBJECTIVES The student should be able to: **1.** List events in England that influenced the writing of the Constitution. **2.** Summarize major compromises needed to draft the Constitution. **3.** Describe Federalist efforts to ratify the Constitution. **4.** Identify problems associated with the Articles of Confederation. **5.** Analyze differences between a Confederation and Federal system of government.

1

1620 ——— MAYFLOWER COMPACT
SIGNED
First written agreement in
America concerning the
making of "just and equal"
laws

During the 1750s, a far more ambitious experiment was devised. Benjamin Franklin's **Albany Plan of Union** proposed a **federal** system of government that would include all the colonies, now thirteen in number. The central authority in Franklin's plan was stronger than the old confederation model. The plan was rejected by the colonies, but it prepared the way for future cooperation among them.

Revolution to Confederation

From the time of the earliest settlements, most colonists had thought of themselves as loyal British subjects. Yet by the 1760s, things had begun to change. The colonists came to believe that the actions of parliament were depriving them of rights and liberties as English citizens. When parliament passed the **Intolerable Acts** in 1772, delegates from the colonies met in Philadelphia to protest the action. The delegates to this **First Continental Congress** debated for nearly two months before agreeing on what to do. They finally demanded that the king respect their rights and allow the colonies **direct representation** in making laws. They also agreed to meet again if the king did not approve their demands.

Shortly thereafter the Revolutionary War began. The delegates reassembled in Philadelphia and assumed the powers of a central government. This **Second Continental Congress** directed the war and drafted a declaration to separate the colonies from England. On July 4, 1776, it approved the final draft of the **Declaration of Independence.**

1643 ——— NEW ENGLAND
CONFEDERATION
APPROVED
English colonies agreed to
form a loose confederation
called The United Colonies of
New England.

The Second Constitutional Convention approved the final draft of the Declaration of Independence on July 4, 1776.

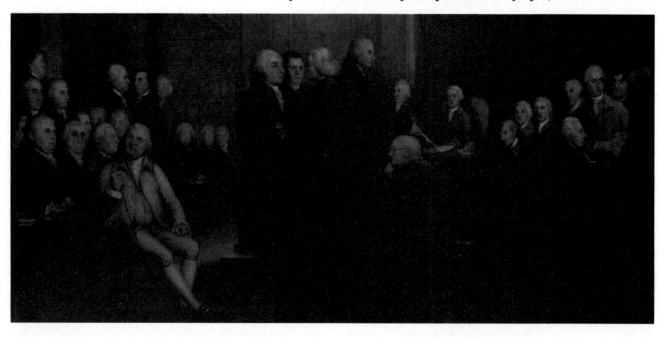

ADDITIONAL MATERIALS Excerpts from the Magna Carta,
Mayflower Compact, Declaration of Independence, and Articles
of Confederation are included on pages T6–T9.

2

Also at this time, a committee was established to draw up a plan of confederation for the colonies. In 1777, the **Articles of Confederation** were presented to Congress and sent to the state legislatures for approval. In 1781, only a few months before the end of the war, the Articles finally went into effect.

Government Under the Articles

Since the thirteen former colonies were wary of centralized authority, the government established by the Articles had very limited powers. It operated through a Congress with one chamber, where each state had a single vote. No chief executive was provided for and no court system was established. The government could not collect taxes, enforce its laws, or regulate trade between states.

As time went on, problems with the Articles became more and more apparent. Conflicts developed between states that the weak central government was unable to resolve. In May 1785, representatives from several states met to iron out differences. They soon agreed that the lack of a central authority was a problem that had to be faced.

In September 1786, a meeting was held in Annapolis, Maryland, to discuss the Articles. The **Annapolis Convention** was only a mixed success. James Madison of Virginia and Alexander Hamilton of New York won support for their plans to make the government stronger. However, only five states sent delegates to the convention, so little could be done. A call for a second convention went out, and Congress soon responded. A constitutional convention was summoned to meet in Philadelphia.

Writing the Constitution

By late May 1787, delegates from every state except Rhode Island had gathered at th Philadelphia convention. The delegates were an impressive group. Franklin, Madison, and Hamilton were among them, and George Washington was elected chairman of the convention. Many of the delegates were lawyers, most had some college education, and all were leaders in their home states.

Despite disagreements on how to proceed with their work, the delegates were agreed on several major points. They wanted a government of *limited* powers. They also wanted a government of *separate* powers: **legislative, executive,** and **judicial.** They wanted the states to have rights, but also to respect the powers of the central government.

Early in the convention, a series of resolutions was introduced that became known as the **Virginia Plan.** The Virginia Plan proposed a government of three branches based on the idea of separation of powers. Large states favored the plan, since it called for a legislature in which states were represented *proportionally,* on the basis of population.

**ENGLISH BILL OF——— 1689
RIGHTS ESTABLISHED**
English king forbidden from suspending the laws and establishes the concept of *habeas corpus.*

POLITICAL SCIENCE   In an early draft of the Declaration of Independence, Thomas Jefferson alluded to the slave trade and accused the King of "suppressing every legislative attempt to prohibit or restrain their execrable commerce." This paragraph was later deleted because of pressure from colonial slaveholders.

Small states opposed the Virginia Plan. They wanted a legislature in which all states were represented *equally.* After some debate, an agreement was reached. The legislature would consist of two houses: a **House of Representatives,** with membership based on state population, and a **Senate,** with each state receiving two members. This agreement became known as the **Connecticut Compromise.**

Throughout the summer of 1787, the delegates worked to complete the new Constitution. Compromises were reached on the matter of counting enslaved Africans for the purposes of representation and taxes and on the issue of government control of trade. At last in September, a final draft was presented to the convention that most of the delegates signed. The Constitution was then sent to the states for approval.

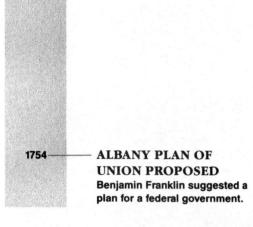

1754 ——— **ALBANY PLAN OF UNION PROPOSED**
Benjamin Franklin suggested a plan for a federal government.

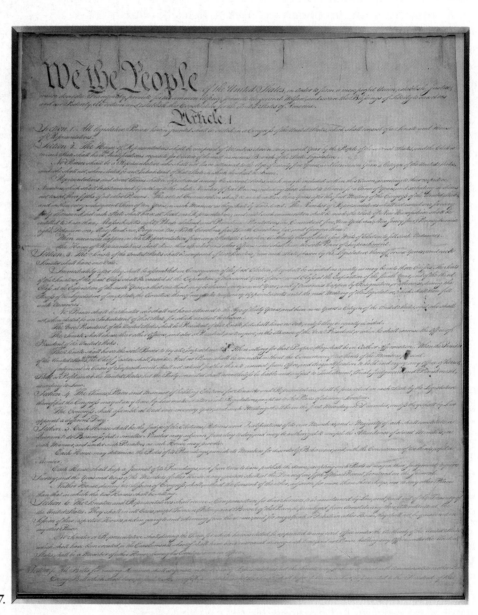

Most delegates to the Constitutional Convention in Philadelphia signed the final draft in September 1787.

HISTORY James Madison frequently offered arguments favoring ratification in the Federalist Papers. Some of his comments from *Federalist #14,* are presented on page T10.

HISTORY Patrick Henry was one of several important people opposed to the Constitution. His concerns are presented in "Anti-Federalist Concerns About the Constitution" on page T11.

The Struggle to Ratify

Nine of the thirteen states had to **ratify** the Constitution before it could take effect. Ratification was not an easy matter, however, because the Constitution had its opponents as well as supporters.

The main supporters of the Constitution were known as **Federalists.** The Federalists argued that a strong central government would protect the new nation from outside interference and also solve internal problems like the regulation of trade. Against them stood the **Anti-Federalists,** led by Samuel Adams of Massachusetts and Patrick Henry of Virginia. The Anti-Federalists feared a strong central government. They believed that power should be distributed among the states, and that a strong central authority would limit personal liberties.

Anti-Federalists were especially concerned that the Constitution lacked a **Bill of Rights.** Federalists argued that a Bill of Rights was not needed, since many state constitutions already provided such protection. To overcome Anti-Federalist objections, however, the Federalists promised to introduce **amendments** that would guarantee personal rights.

The debates over the Constitution provided an opportunity for leading Federalists to clarify many of the ideas the Constitution represented. In a series of essays collectively known as the **Federalist Papers,** Hamilton, Madison, and John Jay argued for the new federal system and outlined the benefits that constitutional government would bring.

In June 1788, New Hampshire became the ninth state to ratify the Constitution. Early in 1789, elections for President were held and the new federal Congress convened in New York, then the nation's temporary capital. On April 30, George Washington was sworn in as the first constitutionally elected President of the United States.

One final piece of work remained to be done. A Bill of Rights had been promised both to the states and to the Anti-Federalists; Congress set about providing one. Amendments to the Constitution were introduced to protect the rights of individuals against the newly-strengthened central government. Ten of these amendments were finally adopted alleviating tensions between Federalists and Anti-Federalists. In November 1791, the new Bill of Rights went into effect. The work of the framers was now complete.

FIRST CONTINENTAL CONGRESS MEETS
Asked the king to give colonists direct representation in making laws

SECOND CONTINENTAL CONGRESS MEETS
Began drafting a declaration of independence from the English crown

DECLARATION OF INDEPENDENCE SIGNED
Document declared independence.

ARTICLES OF CONFEDERATION ADOPTED
States agreed to cooperate with one another for mutual defense and the general good.

MT. VERNON CONFERENCE HELD
Decided that the Articles of Confederation needed revision

ANNAPOLIS CONVENTION HELD
Convention requested Congress to call for a constitutional meeting.

CONSTITUTIONAL CONVENTION MEETS
Delegates met in Philadelphia and produced a federal Constitution for the United States.

FEDERALIST PAPERS WRITTEN
Series of letters supported the ratification of the Constitution.

CONSTITUTION RATIFIED
The Constitution went into effect.

BILL OF RIGHTS ADOPTED
The first ten amendments to the Constitution became law, guaranteeing certain individual rights.

1774
1775
1776

1781

1785
1786
1787
1788

1791

ADDITIONAL MATERIALS The votes of each state for and against the Constitution can be seen on Chart 1, "Ratification Votes for the Constitution," on page T12.

5

ADDITIONAL MATERIALS Use Worksheets 1 and 2 on pages T22 and T23 in conjunction with this lesson.

Profile: James Madison

James Madison is often called the "father of the Constitution." Born in 1751 to a Virginia farm couple, Madison was the oldest of twelve children. In 1769 he entered college and graduated two years later. When signs of revolution appeared in the colonies, Madison became a firm supporter of independence.

In the 1770s Madison entered politics and was soon elected to the Virginia assembly. In 1780 he joined the Continental Congress, at twenty-nine the Congress's youngest member. He thought the Articles of Confederation too weak, and became a leader of the group that favored a strong central government.

During the 1780s Madison worked to have the Articles amended. When the Constitutional Convention met in Philadelphia in May 1787, Madison became one of its most influential members. His notes on the Convention, which met in closed sessions, are a major source of information about what took place there.

Early in the Convention, Madison introduced a plan of federal organization, the Virginia Plan, that soon became the main focus of debate. Later, after a draft Constitution had been approved, he began working for its ratification. With Alexander Hamilton and John Jay, he wrote a series of essays, collectively known as the **Federalist Papers,** that stressed the advantages constitutional government would bring. The essays were widely read, and won the Constitution many new supporters.

In 1788 Madison was elected to the House of Representatives. There he proposed a series of amendments to the new Constitution that came to form the Bill of Rights. When Thomas Jefferson became President in 1801, Madison was appointed secretary of state. Finally, in 1808, at the end of Jefferson's second term, Madison himself was elected President.

Problems with England plagued the Madison presidency. In 1812 war was declared, and in 1814 Madison himself narrowly escaped capture when the British burned Washington.

In 1817 Madison retired to private life. He later succeeded his friend Jefferson as head of the University of Virginia. James Madison died in 1836. Former President John Quincy Adams summed up his importance this way: "It was to the mind of Madison that the union owed its existence."

REVIEW

1. Why was it important that Madison kept notes on the Constitutional Convention?

2. What did John Quincy Adams mean when he said that the United States owed its existence to Madison's mind?

Madison created the Virginia Plan, which called for three branches of government and the separation of powers.

★ ★ ★ ★ LESSON 2 ★ ★ ★ ★
The Legislature

The Constitution was written with the Declaration of Independence in mind. The connection comes out most strongly in the introduction to the Constitution known as the **Preamble.** Like the Declaration, the Preamble is concerned with liberty, and places responsibility for government in the hands of "We the People."

Article I, Sections 1–6 set up a federal legislature. The framers of the Constitution were concerned that states as well as individuals should receive fair representation in making the nation's laws. Article I shows how these concerns were finally resolved.

PREAMBLE

The **Preamble** states the purpose of the Constitution. It proposes a government based on the will of the people who are governed by it. The idea of people governing themselves is known as **direct democracy.** But the system of government set forth in the Constitution is not direct democracy in its purest form. Americans do not vote on everything that affects their welfare. Instead the will of the people is expressed through representatives elected *by* the people. The idea of **representative democracy** is established at very the beginning of the Constitution, in Article I.

WE THE PEOPLE of the United States, in Order to form a more perfect Union, establish justice, insure domestic tranquility, provide for the common defense, promote the general welfare, and secure the blessings of liberty to ourselves and our posterity, do ordain and establish this Constitution for the United States of America.

ARTICLE I

SECTION 1: Congress

A congress can be any assembly or group of individuals. But in the narrow sense used here, **Congress** is an assembly empowered to make laws for the nation. The powers of Congress to make laws are known as **legislative powers.** In our three-branch system of government, only the legislative branch can exercise these powers.

The United States Congress is made up of two houses—the **Senate** and the **House of Representatives.**

SECTION 1

All legislative powers herein granted shall be vested in a Congress of the United States, which shall consist of a Senate and House of Representatives.

OBJECTIVES The student should be able to: **1.** Recognize the main objective of the Preamble.   **2.** List the qualifications for a representative and for a senator.   **3.** Explain how representation in the House and Senate are determined.   **4.** Know the lengths

7

of term of a representative and senator.   **5.** Summarize the privileges and restrictions placed on members of the House and Senate.

SECTION 2

1. The House of Representatives shall be composed of members chosen every second year by the people of the several states, and the electors in each state shall have the qualifications requisite for electors of the most numerous branch of the state legislature.

2. No person shall be a representative who shall not have attained to the age of twenty-five years, and been seven years a citizen of the United States, and who shall not, when elected, be an inhabitant of that state in which he shall be chosen.

SECTION 2: House of Representatives

1. *Election and term of office.* Members of the House are elected for a term of two years. Since representatives' terms do not overlap, all candidates for the House stand for election at the same time. Representatives are elected directly by the voters of each state, though who those voters are exactly the Constitution does not make clear. Qualifications for voting were left to the individual states. But different states adopted different voting requirements, which sometimes created problems. Today, most states have adopted three requirements for voting for representatives. Voters must be United States citizens; they must fulfill certain terms of residency; and they must be registered to vote. Several amendments have also changed our understanding of this section of the Constitution. **Amendments 15, 19, 24,** and **26** have limited the states' powers to determine who can and cannot vote.

2. *Qualifications for membership.* Requirements for membership in the House are less demanding than for membership in the Senate. Representatives must be at least twenty-five years old and have been citizens of the United States for at least seven years. They must also live in the state they represent at the time of their election. They do not have to live in the district they represent, but few House candidates run for election outside their home district.

The Senate and the House of Representatives meet in the Capitol in Washington, D.C.

POLITICAL SCIENCE   The French political philosopher Montesquieu originally put forth the concept of three branches of government in *The Spirit of Laws,* published in 1748.

8

3. *Number of representatives for each state.* Population determines the number of representatives each state will have. To ensure a fair distribution of House seats, the Constitution specified that the population must be counted every ten years. This population counting is called a **census.** Most states have several representatives, but *every* state, regardless of population, is entitled to at least one.

The passage referring to "three-fifths of all other persons" was included in the Constitution to deal with the problem of how to count enslaved Africans for purposes of representation. When **Amendment 13** abolished slavery, this passage ceased to have any meaning.

As the population increased, the number of seats in the House continued to grow. In 1929 Congress passed a law limiting the total number of representatives to 435.

4. *Vacancies in the House.* If a representative dies, gives up his or her seat, or is removed from office, the state governor is required to call an election to fill the vacant seat.

5. *Choosing officers and impeachment.* The Constitution specifies only that the House will choose a speaker, not what the powers of the speaker will be. But in practice the Speaker of the House has been a powerful fixture. The speaker presides over meetings of the House, enforces its rules, and determines when individual members may speak. By an act of Congress, the Speaker of the House follows only the Vice-President in line of succession to the presidency. In theory the speaker does not have to be a member of the House, but in fact always is. The speaker invariably comes from the party with the most seats in the House.

The Constitution gives the House "the sole power of impeachment." To **impeach** means to accuse a government official of wrongdoing. The House can bring impeachment charges against the President, Vice-President, and other officers of government. It cannot bring charges against any member of Congress. But the House only has the power to *accuse.* The power to conduct a trial of impeachment voted by the House belongs solely to the Senate. (See **Article II, Section 4.**)

3. Representatives and direct taxes shall be apportioned among the several states which may be included within this Union, according to their respective numbers, which shall be determined by adding to the whole number of free persons, including those bound to service for a term of years, and excluding Indians not taxed, three-fifths of all other persons. The actual enumeration shall be made within three years after the first meeting of the Congress of the United States, and within every subsequent term of ten years, in such manner as they shall by law direct. The number of representatives shall not exceed one for every thirty thousand, but each state shall have at least one representative; and until such enumeration shall be made, the state of New Hampshire shall be entitled to choose 3, Massachusetts 8, Rhode Island and Providence Plantations 1, Connecticut 5, New York 6, New Jersey 4, Pennsylvania 8, Delaware 1, Maryland 6, Virginia 10, North Carolina 5, South Carolina 5, and Georgia 3.

4. When vacancies happen in the representation from any state, the executive authority thereof shall issue writs of election to fill such vacancies.

5. The House of Representatives shall choose their speaker and other officers; and shall have the sole power of impeachment.

HISTORY Early twentieth-century historian, Charles Beard, noted that many of the men who drew up the Constitution were from the wealthy, property-owning aristocracy. He felt that while they did not seek personal gain, they did have direct economic interests in a strong federal government.

SECTION 3

1. The Senate of the United States shall be composed of two senators from each state, chosen by the legislature thereof, for six years; and each senator shall have one vote.

2. Immediately after they shall be assembled in consequence of the first election, they shall be divided as equally as may be into three classes. The seats of the senators of the first class shall be vacated at the expiration of the second year, of the second class at the expiration of the fourth year, and of the third class at the expiration of the sixth year, so that one third may be chosen every second year; and if vacancies happen by resignation, or otherwise, during the recess of the legislature of any state, the executive thereof may make temporary appointments until the next meeting of the legislature, which shall then fill such vacancies.

3. No person shall be a senator who shall not have attained to the age of thirty years, and been nine years a citizen of the United States, and who shall not, when elected, be an inhabitant of that state for which he shall be chosen.

4. The Vice President of the United States shall be president of the Senate, but shall have no vote, unless they be equally divided.

5. The Senate shall choose their other officers, and also a president **pro tempore,** in the absence of the Vice President, or when he shall exercise the office of President of the United States.

SECTION 3: Senate

1. *Selection of members.* In the Senate states are represented *equally* rather than proportionally. Every state is entitled to two Senate members, regardless of population.

Senators serve a term of six years. Originally senators were chosen by the legislatures of their states. But since 1913, as required by **Amendment 17,** senators have been elected directly by the voters of each state.

2. *Terms and vacancies.* Elections for the Senate are staggered. One-third of the Senate stands for election every two years. This provides the Senate with a continuity of membership that the House of Representatives does not have.

The last part of this passage has been amended. **Amendment 17** specifies that if a Senate seat falls vacant, the state governor will appoint a temporary senator until an election can be held.

3. *Qualifications for membership.* Qualifications for the Senate are more rigorous than qualifications for the House. Senators must be at least thirty years old when they take the oath of office. They must also have been citizens of the United States for at least nine years and live in the state they represent.

4. *President of the Senate.* Presiding over the Senate is the Vice-President's only constitutionally specified duty. In Senate debates, the Vice-President casts a vote only in the case of a tie. Since ties rarely occur, the Vice-President seldom exercises this power.

5. *Election of officers.* The Senate selects its officers from its own membership. It also chooses a **president pro tempore,** or temporary president, to preside over sessions when the Vice-President is absent. The president pro tempore has much the same role in the Senate as the speaker does in the House. In line of succession to the presidency, the president pro tempore follows only the Vice-President and the Speaker of the House.

HISTORY At the Constitutional Convention, Alexander Hamilton proposed that both the President and members of the Senate hold office for life.

6. *Impeachment trials.* Although the House of Representatives has the sole power of impeachment, it is the Senate that conducts the actual impeachment trial. If the President of the United States is impeached, the Chief Justice of the Supreme Court presides over his trial. Conviction on impeachment charges requires a two-thirds vote of the senators present at the time of the voting.

Only two sitting Presidents have been impeached. In 1868, the House impeached Andrew Johnson. Over one hundred years later, in 1998, President Bill Clinton was impeached. Neither President, however, was convicted by the Senate. In 1974, a committee in the House recommended the President Richard Nixon be impeached, but Nixon resigned before the full House could vote on his impeachment.

7. *Impeachment convictions.* An impeachment conviction does not carry with it any criminal penalties. A convicted official can only be removed from office and banned from holding other offices. Once removed, however, the convicted official is subject to normal criminal proceedings and punishments. **Article II, Section 4** spells out offenses for which officials can be impeached.

6. The Senate shall have the sole power to try all impeachments. When sitting for that purpose, they shall be on oath or affirmation. When the President of the United States is tried, the Chief Justice shall preside: and no person shall be convicted without the concurrence of two-thirds of the members present.

7. Judgement in cases of impeachment shall not extend further than to removal from office, and disqualification to hold and enjoy any office of honor, trust or profit under the United States: but the party convicted shall nevertheless be liable and subject to indictment, trial, judgment and punishment, according to law.

A joint session of Congress

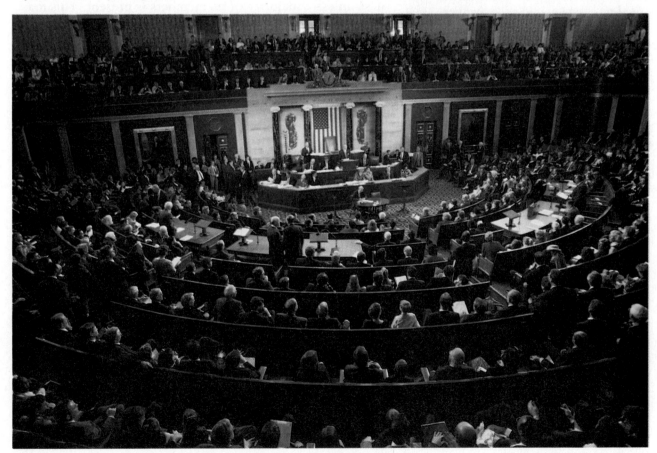

HISTORY Eight different resolutions for Nixon's impeachment were introduced into the House by the fall of 1973. It was not until August 1974 that he heeded advice and resigned.

ADDITIONAL MATERIALS Events leading to Nixon's resignation are discussed in "Case Study: United States v Nixon" on page 28.

SECTION 4

1. The times, places and manner of holding elections for senators and representatives, shall be prescribed in each state by the legislature thereof; but the Congress may at any time by law make or alter such regulations, except as to the places of choosing senators.

2. The Congress shall assemble at least once in every year, and such meeting shall be on the first Monday in December, unless they shall by law appoint a different day.

SECTION 5

1. Each house shall be the judge of elections, returns and qualifications of its own members, and a majority of each shall constitute a quorum to do business; but a smaller number may adjourn from day to day, and may be authorized to compel the attendance of absent members, in such manner, and under such penalties as each house may provide.

2. Each house may determine the rules of its proceedings, punish its members for disorderly behavior, and, with the concurrence of two-thirds, expel a member.

3. Each house shall keep a journal of its proceedings, and from time to time publish the same, excepting such parts as may in their judgment require secrecy; and the yeas and nays of the members of either house on any question shall, at the desire of one-fifth of those present, be entered on the journal.

SECTION 4: Elections and Meetings

1. *Electing members to Congress.* The Constitution gives state legislatures the power to control the elections of their own members to Congress. But Congress can interfere with this power when necessary, and has done so in significant ways. For example, Congress has required the states to elect their representatives by districts, and has set a standard date for all congressional elections.

2. *Annual meetings.* Congress must meet at least once every year. But the opening date of the congressional session has been changed by **Amendment 20.** Congress must now convene on January 3, unless a different date is set by law.

SECTION 5: Rules of Business in Congress

1. *Organization.* Each house of Congress decides whether its members are properly elected and qualified to serve. Each house may refuse to seat a newly elected member, but only if the member does not meet constitutional requirements of age, citizenship, or residency.

Neither house may vote on bills or conduct other business unless a majority of its members is present. This majority constitutes a **quorum,** the minimum number of members needed before an organization can act. In order to form a quorum and for other reasons, Congress can require members' attendance at its meetings.

2. *Rules.* Each house of Congress sets its own rules and procedures. Rules for both houses are often similar, though sometimes they differ in significant ways. For example, the House imposes a strict limit on how long members may speak, but the Senate allows its members to speak for as long as they see fit.

Members of either house can be punished if they break the rules of the house or become disorderly. They can also be expelled from the house by a two-thirds vote of its members.

3. *Keeping an official record.* Each house must keep an official journal of its meetings. These journals are published at the end of a congressional session. The journals list all bills presented during the session as well as the votes of individual members. But matters involving national security may be left out of the published record if either house so chooses.

4. *Rules for adjournment.* Once a session of Congress has started, neither house can adjourn for more than three days without the consent of the other house. Nor can one house move its place of meeting—to another city, for example—without similar consent.

SECTION 6: Privileges and Restrictions

1. *Congressional salaries and privileges.* Senators and representatives are paid out of the United States Treasury. Their salaries are set by law and periodically revised.

Members cannot be tried or sued for anything they say on the floor of Congress or in congressional committees. They also enjoy some immunity from criminal arrest, though they can be arrested, tried, and convicted for murder, robbery, and other criminal offenses.

2. *Employment restrictions.* As long as they are members of Congress, senators and representatives cannot hold any other federal office or employment. Nor can they at a later date accept any federal job created while they were members, or any *emoluments*—salaries, raises, and other benefits—voted during their term of office.

4. Neither house, during the session of Congress, shall, without the consent of the other, adjourn for more than three days, nor to any other place than that in which the two houses shall be sitting.

SECTION 6

1. The senators and representatives shall receive a compensation for their services, to be ascertained by law, and paid out of the treasury of the United States. They shall in all cases, except treason, felony and breach of the peace, be privileged from arrest during their attendance at the session of their respective houses, and in going to and returning from the same; and for any speech or debate in either house, they shall not be questioned in any other place.

2. No senator or representative shall, during the time for which he was elected, be appointed to any civil office under the authority of the United States, which shall have been created, or the emoluments whereof shall have been increased during such time; and no person holding any office under the United States, shall be a member of either house during his continuance in office.

The Constitution gives Congress the power to establish its own rules. This picture shows the House of Representatives conducting business according to these rules.

ADDITIONAL MATERIALS   Use Worksheets 3 and 4 on pages T24 and T25 in conjunction with this lesson.

Case Study: The Impeachment Trial of Andrew Johnson

On April 15, 1865, the morning after the assassination of President Abraham Lincoln, Vice-President Andrew Johnson was sworn in as President. The new President faced a difficult task. The Civil War had only recently ended, and opinion was divided on how to deal with the defeated South. Like Lincoln, Johnson favored leniency. He supported a plan of **Reconstruction** that would bring the South back into the union peacefully.

The radicals who controlled the Republican Party were opposed to this lenient approach. They wanted to set up military governments in the South that would punish the rebel states and keep their own party in power.

The President and the radical-led Congress were soon openly at odds. Congress refused to accept the President's Reconstruction program, while the President regularly vetoed radical-sponsored bills. In March 1867, to protect its power against "executive tyranny," Congress passed the **Tenure of Office Act.** The act forbade the President to remove federal officials who were previously confirmed by Congress without congressional consent. To test this act, which he considered unconstitutional and had already tried to veto, Johnson dismissed his radical secretary of war, Edwin M. Stanton. The radicals charged that the President had broken the law, and the House voted to impeach.

The impeachment trial began in the Senate in March 1868 and lasted over two months. In many ways the issues involved were more political and personal than constitutional. Still the basic idea of **separation of powers** was at stake: Congress wanted to control the President's actions, and the President wanted to act as he thought proper.

On May 16 the senators came to a vote on the most serious impeachment charge. Thirty-five voted to convict, nineteen to acquit. Since the vote fell one short of the two-thirds majority needed to convict, the President was found not guilty. Ten days later he was acquitted on lesser charges as well.

The sergeant-at-arms of the House hands Johnson (at right) a bill of impeachment. Johnson's acquittal reaffirmed the principle of separation of powers.

The effects of the impeachment verdict were far reaching. The powers of the presidency were secured against congressional interference, and the independence of the executive and legislature was reaffirmed. In the end, the constitutional machinery performed exactly as the framers had intended. It showed that a federal model could function in spite of tensions between its separate parts.

REVIEW

1. What was the real reason why Andrew Johnson was impeached?

2. What Article and Section in the Constitution gives Congress the power to impeach? What does it say?

14

★ ★ ★ ★ LESSON 3 ★ ★ ★ ★
Making Laws

In **Section 7** the framers set out the process for passing laws. Because the states feared a strong federal government, Section 7 also introduces a system of checks and balances. **Sections 8** and **9** limit the power of Congress more, but **Section 10** limits the states.

ARTICLE I

SECTION 7: Passing Laws

1. *Raising money.* To prevent "taxation without representation," only the "people's representatives" can propose tax laws. Under the system of checks and balances, however, the Senate can propose amendments.

2. *How a bill becomes law.* The rules for passing a law are probably the most important place that we see the system of checks and balances. Both houses of Congress must pass a **bill,** or proposed law. Then the President must sign the bill before it becomes law.

The President can **veto** or refuse to sign a bill, however. This lets the President "check" the power of Congress. A vetoed bill is sent back to the house where it was introduced with a written statement of the President's objections. This statement is then entered into the *Congressional Record.*

When a bill is returned, Congress has the right to reconsider it. If **two-thirds** of each house approves the bill, it becomes law, even though the President has vetoed it. This is another place where checks and balances can be seen. In this case, Congress can "check" the President's power to veto a bill.

A bill may become a law in another way, however. If the President receives a bill but *does not* sign or veto it within ten days (excluding Sundays), the bill automatically becomes a law. Presidents have used this method to allow bills they really do not like to become law.

If Congress adjourns during the ten-day period, however, the bill *does not* become a law. This is called a **pocket veto,** because the bill has, in effect, been kept in the President's pocket until Congress adjourned.

SECTION 7

1. All bills for raising revenue shall originate in the House of Representatives; but the Senate may propose or concur with amendments as on other bills.

2. Every bill which shall have passed the House of Representatives and the Senate, shall, before it become a law, be presented to the President of the United States; if he approve he shall sign it, but if not he shall return it, with his objections to that house in which it shall have originated, who shall enter the objections at large on their journal, and proceed to reconsider it. If after such reconsideration two-thirds of that house shall agree to pass the bill, it shall be sent, together with the objections, to the other house, by which it shall likewise be reconsidered, and if approved by two-thirds of that house, it shall become a law. But in all such cases the votes of both houses shall be determined by yeas and nays, and the names of the persons voting for and against the bill shall be entered on the journal of each house respectively. If any bill shall not be returned by the President within ten days (Sundays excepted) after it shall have been presented to him, the same shall be a law, in like manner as if he had signed it, unless the Congress by their adjournment prevent its return, in which case it shall not be a law.

3. Every order, resolution, or vote to which the concurrence of the Senate and House of Representatives may be necessary (except on a question of adjournment) shall be presented to the President of the United States; and before the same shall take effect, shall be approved by him, or being disapproved by him, shall be repassed by two-thirds of the Senate and House of Representatives, according to the rules and limitations prescribed in the case of a bill.

SECTION 8

1. The Congress shall have power: To lay and collect taxes, duties, imposts and excises, to pay the debts and provide for the common defense and general welfare of the United States; but all duties, imposts and excises shall be uniform throughout the United States;

2. To borrow money on the credit of the United States;

3. To regulate commerce with foreign nations, and among the several states, and with the Indian tribes;

4. To establish an uniform rule of naturalization, and uniform laws on the subject of bankruptcies throughout the United States;

3. *President can approve or disapprove congressional actions.* Any other agreement between the two houses, except to adjourn, must be approved by the President. This keeps Congress from bypassing the President's power to "check" Congress.

SECTION 8: Powers Given to Congress

Because the framers remained suspicious of powerful government, they listed the **enumerated powers,** so-called because they are "numbered and listed."

1. *To tax and pay debts.* The power to tax lets Congress pay the government's debts, provide services to the people, and defend the nation. Even though this is often seen as giving Congress unlimited authority, the power to tax is limited. Export taxes, for example, are specifically prohibited by the Constitution.

2. *To borrow money.* Congress can borrow money to run the government.

3. *To regulate trade.* This "commerce clause" gives Congress broad power to regulate trade.

4. *Naturalization and bankruptcies.* Congress can pass laws about **naturalization** (making foreigners U.S. citizens) and **bankruptcies** (businesses and individuals who cannot pay their debts).

Naturalization laws passed by Congress have allowed millions of immigrants to become U.S. citizens.

5. *Money, weights, and measures.* Congress can make money, decide its worth in terms of foreign money, and set a national system of weights and measures. (All these powers simplify trade.)

6. *Counterfeiting.* Congress can make laws to punish printers of counterfeit (fake) money and other items.

7. *A postal service.* Congress can create a postal service and roads needed for delivering the mail.

8. *Copyrights and patents.* Congress can pass laws granting **copyrights,** exclusive rights to sell literary, musical, or artistic works. Congress can also pass laws that grant **patents,** exclusive rights to use inventions.

9. *Other courts.* Congress can create federal courts that are less powerful than the Supreme Court.

10. *Crimes at sea.* Congress can make laws about crimes committed in any waters where U.S. ships are involved.

11. *Declarations of war.* Only Congress can declare war. Not all wars have been declared, though. To find out more, read the case study, "The 'War Powers Act.' "

12. *Create and support an army.* Defense was an important reason for forming a union of states. Congress has used this power to enact a military **draft** at various times. In 1973, however, Congress ended the draft.

13. *Create and support a navy.* Today the U.S. Navy is one of the largest in the world.

14. *Make rules for the military.* Congress can establish rules to govern the military.

15. *Command state militia (national guards).* In emergencies, the federal government can take control of the state militia from the state's governor.

16. *To regulate state national guards.* Congress makes the basic rules that govern state militia. Although each state has the right to appoint officers, it is responsible for carrying out the rules laid down by Congress.

5. To coin money, regulate the value thereof, and of foreign coin, and fix the standard of weights and measures;

6. To provide for the punishment of counterfeiting the securities and current coin of the United States;

7. To establish post offices and post roads;

8. To promote the progress of science and useful arts, by securing for limited times to authors and inventors the exclusive right to their respective writings and discoveries;

9. To constitute tribunals inferior to the Supreme Court;

10. To define and punish piracies and felonies committed on the high seas, and offenses against the law of nations;

11. To declare war, grant letters of marque and reprisal, and make rules concerning captures on land and water;

12. To raise and support armies, but no appropriation of money to that use shall be for a longer term than two years;

13. To provide and maintain a navy;

14. To make rules for the government and regulation of the land and naval forces;

15. To provide for calling forth the militia to execute the laws of the Union, suppress insurrections and repel invasions;

16. To provide for organizing, arming, and disciplining, the militia, and for governing such part of them as may be employed in the service of the United States, reserving to the states respectively, the appointment of the officers, and the authority of training the militia according to the discipline prescribed by Congress;

POLITICAL SCIENCE The Constitution stipulates only a Supreme Court and "such inferior courts as the Congress may . . . establish." One of the first acts of Congress was to establish a federal court system.

17

17. To exercise exclusive legislation in all cases whatsoever, over such district (not exceeding ten miles square) as may, by cession of particular states, and the acceptance of Congress, become the seat of the government of the United States, and to exercise like authority over all places purchased by the consent of the legislature of the state in which the same shall be, for the erection of forts, magazines, arsenals, dockyards, and other needful buildings;—And

18. To make all laws which shall be necessary and proper for carrying into execution the foregoing powers, and all other powers vested by this Constitution in the government of the United States, or in any department or officer thereof.

SECTION 9

1. The migration or importation of such persons as any of the states now existing shall think proper to admit, shall not be prohibited by the Congress prior to the year one thousand eight hundred and eight, but a tax or duty may be imposed on such importation, not exceeding ten dollars for each person.

2. The privilege of the writ of **habeas corpus** shall not be suspended, unless when in cases of rebellion or invasion the public safety may require it.

3. No bill of attainder or **ex post facto** law shall be passed.

4. No capitation, [or other direct,] tax shall be laid, unless in proportion to the census or enumeration herein before directed to be taken.

5. No tax or duty shall be laid on articles exported from any state.

17. *To establish the capital city and federally owned lands.* This gave Congress the power to establish a capital for the federal government. In 1790, Washington, District of Columbia, was suggested as the capital's location. Since the majority of the population lived along the Atlantic seacoast, Congress agreed. Washington also had the advantage of being centrally located between the North and South. Further, Maryland and Virginia agreed to donate the site to the federal government. Congress also has the power to make laws for Washington, D.C., and for any other federal property, such as military bases.

18. *To make laws needed to carry out the Constitution and govern the nation.* The framers expected the future to bring conditions they had not foreseen. They wanted to let Congress carry out its duties, without being limited by the "enumerated powers." This **elastic clause** lets Congress expand its powers as needed.

SECTION 9: Powers Denied to Congress

1. *Slave trading.* This clause was part of the compromise between the slave-holding states of the South and the nonslave states of the North. The Southern states were allowed to import enslaved people until at least 1808, but they could be required to pay a ten-dollar tax on each one. This clause became obsolete in 1865, when **Amendment 13** outlawed slavery.

2. *Writ of Habeas Corpus.* A **writ of habeas corpus** is an order to bring a prisoner before a judge so that the judge can decide if the prisoner is being held lawfully. If not, the judge can order the prisoner's release.

3. *Bills of attainder and ex post facto laws.* Congress cannot pass a **bill of attainder,** which declares someone guilty without a court trial, or an **ex post facto** law, which makes someone guilty of a crime committed *before* the act was made illegal.

4. *Direct taxes.* Initially, Congress could only pass taxes that were equally divided among the states. Individuals could not be taxed. **Amendment 16** changed this by allowing the individual income tax.

5. *Taxes on exports.* The South approved the commerce clause only when Congress was forbidden to tax exports.

POLITICAL SCIENCE   Through Amendment 10, states may exercise those powers—reserved powers—neither given to the federal government nor prohibited to state governments. These

18

include such activities as conducting elections, regulating hunting and fishing, and licensing of automobile drivers.

6. *State commerce.* All laws regulating commerce must be applied equally to all states. The framers were convinced that free trade between states was crucial to the nation's survival. To encourage such trade, goods shipped **interstate** (between states) cannot be taxed.

7. *Spending money.* No money can be spent until Congress passes a bill allowing it. This clause lets Congress control the money spent by the entire government. The government must also publish a regular accounting of all money it takes in and spends. Today this duty is fulfilled by the President's annual budget.

8. *Titles of nobility.* With the experience of royal power fresh in their minds, the framers prohibited titles of nobility, such as king. Unless Congress allows it, federal officials cannot accept gifts from foreign countries, for fear the gift would act as a **bribe.** Large gifts from foreign countries have been accepted, but only in the name of the United States.

SECTION 10: Powers Denied to the States
1. *Treaties, coinage, and laws.* A big problem under the Articles of Confederation was that the states acted on their own. To be sure the nation acts as a unit, no state can sign a treaty with another country. The money many states printed was another problem. Because the resulting confusion hurt trade, no state can print money. To further protect **free enterprise,** trade that is free of government restraint, no state can pass laws that interfere with contracts, the basis of trade.

2. *Taxes on imports and exports.* Since the national government was given exclusive power over trade, the states cannot tax imported or exported goods. Over the years, some states have been given the right to charge an "inspection fee" on goods coming into them. Any money collected for inspection must be turned over to the federal government, however.

3. *Duties, the military, and declarations of war.* States cannot tax ships or how much they carry, unless Congress gives permission. Neither can states engage in war or make peace. The only exception is if a state is being invaded or is in immediate danger of being invaded.

6. No preference shall be given by any regulation of commerce or revenue to the ports of one state over those of another: nor shall vessels bound to, or from, one state, be obliged to enter, clear, or pay duties in another.

7. No money shall be drawn from the treasury, but in consequence of appropriations made by law; and a regular statement and account of the receipts and expenditures of all public money shall be published from time to time.

8. No title of nobility shall be granted by the United States: And no person holding any office of profit or trust under them, shall, without the consent of the Congress, accept of any present, emolument, office, or title, of any kind whatever, from any king, prince, or foreign state.

SECTION 10
1. No state shall enter into any treaty, alliance, or confederation; grant letters of marque and reprisal; coin money; emit bills of credit; make anything but gold and silver coin a tender in payment of debts; pass any bill of attainder, **ex post facto** law, or law impairing the obligation of contracts, or grant any title of nobility.

2. No state shall, without the consent of Congress, lay any imposts or duties on imports or exports, except what may be absolutely necessary for executing its inspection laws: and the net produce of all duties and imposts, laid by any state on imports or exports, shall be for the use of the treasury of the United States, and all such laws shall be subject to the revision and control of the Congress.

3. No state shall, without the consent of Congress, lay any duty of tonnage, keep troops, or ships of war in time of peace, enter into any agreement or compact with another state, or with a foreign power, or engage in war, unless actually invaded, or in such imminent danger as will not admit of delay.

Case Study: The "War Powers Act"

"The Congress shall have Power to declare War. . . ." Constitution, Art. II, Sec. 8, Clause 11

With the Constitution, the framers hoped to solve the problems of British rule. One of these was the King's misuse of the military. Without the people's consent, he quartered troops, drafted soldiers, and engaged in war.

Because an army can have only one leader, the framers named the President commander in chief of the armed forces. Congress, however, received exclusive power to declare war and provide money for the military.

In theory, then, Congress controls the military. Without a declaration, wars cannot be fought. Without money, battles cannot be launched. Nevertheless, the United States has sent troops to foreign countries more than 160 times since 1789, but Congress has only declared war five times. Most have been military actions ordered by the President, acting as commander in chief to protect national interests.

One of these military actions was Vietnam, where more than eight million Americans fought. The United States began sending help to Vietnam as early as 1950. Then, in 1965, President Johnson ordered troops to South Vietnam to protect its government. Congress never declared war, but U.S. involvement grew and grew. Finally, in 1973, President Nixon ordered U.S. troops home.

Fighting in Vietnam sparked great social and political unrest in the United States. To limit the President's power to make war, Congress passed the **War Powers Act** in 1973. If the President orders troops to foreign lands, Congress must be informed within forty-eight hours. If Congress does not approve the action or declare war within ninety days, the troops must come home.

Supporters of the act said it simply confirms the constitutional powers of Congress. Opponents argued that it limits the President's ability to respond to emergencies. Some think the act is unconstitutional. The controversy continues and may not be settled unless it is put before the Supreme Court.

REVIEW

1. Why did Congress feel it needed to pass the War Powers Act?

2. Name as many wars in which Americans have fought as you can.

3. In your opinion, should the President's power to use troops be limited? Why?

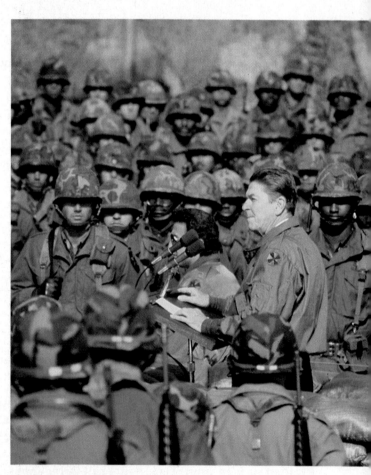

President Reagan reviews the troops. Although the President is commander in chief of the armed forces, only Congress has the constitutional right to declare war.

REVIEW ANSWERS 1. To impose a limit on the President's power to make war or conduct military actions. 2. Possible answers include: Revolutionary War, War of 1812, Mexican War, Civil War, Spanish American War, World Wars I and II, Korean War, Vietnam War. 3. Answers will vary. Students should include logical support for their opinions.

20

Name _____

REVIEW 1
Lessons 1–3

A. VOCABULARY—PREAMBLE AND ARTICLE I

In the space after each question, write the correct word *and* where the word is used in the Constitution.

1. The second goal in the Constitution's introduction. _____ Justice; Preamble. _____

2. This is a person's exclusive right to publish and sell literary, musical, or artistic works.
   _____ Copyright; Sec. 8, Cl. 8 _____

3. A member of Congress's larger house serves a two-year term.
   _____ Representative; Sec. 2, Cl. 1 _____

4. This official count of the population occurs every ten years. _____ Census; Sec. 2, Cl. 3 _____

5. The Vice-President has this title in the Senate. _____ President pro tempore; Sec. 3, Cl. 4 _____

6. This is a proposed law. _____ Bill; Sec. 7, Cl. 1 _____

7. This happens when the President refuses to sign a bill. _____ Veto; Sec. 7, Cl. 1 _____

8. These are specific powers given to Congress. _____ Enumerated powers; Sec. 8, Cl. 1–17 _____

9. Only Congress can make laws that require these payments to the federal government.
   _____ Taxes; Sec. 8, Cl. 1 _____

10. This passage lets Congress expand its powers as needed to carry out its duties.
    _____ Elastic clause; Sec. 8, Cl. 18 _____

11. This distributes seats in the House of Representatives on the basis of state population.
    _____ Apportionment; Sec. 1, Cl. 3 _____

12. This member of the smaller house of Congress is elected for a six-year term.
    _____ Senator; Sec. 3, Cl. 1 _____

B. CRITICAL THINKING

1. List several arguments in favor of ratifying the Constitution. What was the main fear of those who opposed it?
   A strong central government would protect the United States from
   outside interference and solve internal problems such as the
   regulation of trade. The people who opposed the Constitution feared
   that a strong central government would limit personal liberties.

21

2. Explain the main difference between the confederation established under the Articles of Confederation and the federal system established under the Constitution.

Under the Confederation, the central government had very little

authority; there was no chief executive and no national court

system; the government could not collect taxes or regulate trade

between the states. The new Constitution created a strong central

government with a President and court system and gave it the power

to collect taxes and regulate commerce.

_____

_____

C. FACTS AND IDEAS

On the line to the left of each term or power, write the letter that corresponds to the correct section and clause.

TERM OR POWER

E   **1.** Each state has two senators.

B   **2.** Representatives are elected every two years.

O   **3.** This clause lets Congress stretch its powers.

D   **4.** The number of representatives is determined by a census.

M   **5.** It explains how a bill becomes a law.

F   **6.** One-third of the Senate is elected every two years.

P   **7.** Certain powers are denied to Congress.

H   **8.** Only the Senate may try impeached officials.

I   **9.** Congress must meet at least once every year.

J   **10.** Each house must keep a record of what happens.

K   **11.** Members of Congress cannot hold other government jobs.

C   **12.** Representatives must be at least twenty-five years old.

L   **13.** All tax bills begin in the House of Representatives.

N   **14.** The "enumerated powers" are found here.

Q   **15.** States cannot make war or peace.

A   **16.** Law-making powers belong to Congress.

G   **17.** Senators must be at least thirty years old.

SECTION AND CLAUSE

A. Section 1

B. Section 2, Clause 1

C. Section 2, Clause 2

D. Section 2, Clause 3

E. Section 3, Clause 1

F. Section 3, Clause 2

G. Section 3, Clause 3

H. Section 3, Clause 6

I. Section 4, Clause 2

J. Section 5, Clause 3

K. Section 6, Clause 2

L. Section 7, Clause 1

M. Section 7, Clause 2

N. Section 8, Clauses 1–17

O. Section 8, Clause 18

P. Section 9, Clauses 1–8

Q. Section 10, Clause 3

22

★ ★ ★ ★ LESSON 4 ★ ★ ★ ★
The EXECUTIVE BRANCH

One of the difficult questions facing the framers was that of a chief executive. Clearly, a single leader with broad but limited powers was needed to carry on the daily business of government. Life under King George III had convinced them they did not want a king, though. Rather, the nation needed an elected official who would work for the interests of a majority of the citizens. **Article II, Section 1** sets up a system for electing a President and lists the requirements for holding office. **Sections 2** and **3** define the President's powers and duties. Because the framers feared that officials might abuse their powers, **Section 4** sets up a system for *impeachment,* or formally charging the President or other officials with misconduct. This is another new and unique feature in our Constitution.

ARTICLE II

SECTION 1: President and Vice-President

1. *Term of office.* As the nation's chief executive, the President is responsible for carrying out the laws made by Congress and for upholding the Constitution, the nation's fundamental law.

Most of the framers wanted a strong presidency, believing that strong legislative and judicial branches would be able to "check" the President's power. Others feared a strong executive, however. Finally, the idea of one strong President won out.

The debate then turned to how long a President and Vice-President should serve. Since representatives served for two years, and senators for six, the framers finally compromised on a four-year Presidential term that split the difference. No limit was put on the number of terms, however. After Franklin Roosevelt was elected to a third and then fourth term, an amendment was introduced to limit a President's tenure in office. **Amendment 22** made two terms the legal limit.

SECTION 1

1. The executive power shall be vested in a President of the United States of America. He shall hold his office during the term of four years, and, together with the Vice President, chosen for the same term, be elected, as follows:

John F. Kennedy became the head of the executive branch of government when he became President in 1961.

OBJECTIVES The student should be able to: **1.** Describe the qualifications for President and Vice-President. **2.** List the first four officials to succeed if the President is unable to continue in **23** office. **3.** Understand the meaning of the oath of office taken by the President. **4.** Give examples of some of the powers of the President. **5.** Indicate the duties of the President.

2. Each state shall appoint, in such manner as the legislature thereof may direct, a number of electors, equal to the whole number of senators and representatives to which the state may be entitled in the Congress: but no senator or representative, or person holding an office of trust or profit under the United States, shall be appointed an elector.

3. The electors shall meet in their respective states, and vote by ballot for two persons, of whom one at least shall not be an inhabitant of the same state with themselves. And they shall make a list of all the persons voted for, and of the number of votes for each; which list they shall sign and certify, and transmit sealed to the seat of the government of the United States, directed to the president of the Senate. The president of the Senate shall, in the presence of the Senate and House of Representatives, open all the certificates, and the votes shall then be counted. The person having the greatest number of votes shall be the President, if such number be a majority of the whole number of electors appointed; and if there be more than one who have such majority, and have an equal number of votes, then the House of Representatives shall immediately choose by ballot one of them for President; and if no person have a majority, then from the five highest on the list the said House shall in like manner choose the President. But in choosing the President, the votes shall be taken by states, the representation from each state having one vote; a quorum for this purpose shall consist of a member or members from two-thirds of the states, and a majority of all the states shall be necessary to a choice. In every case, after the choice of the President, the person having the greatest number of votes of the electors shall be the Vice President. But if there should remain two or more who have equal votes, the Senate shall choose from them by ballot the Vice President.

2. *Electors.* Not all the framers were confident that the common people would do a good job of picking the President and Vice-President. As a result, they set up an indirect system called the Electoral College. When the people voted, they actually chose **electors,** who then voted for the President and Vice-President. Each state was to have as many electors as it had members in Congress. Electors were selected by state legislatures, who decided who was eligible. Originally no individual who already held federal office could be an elector.

3. *Election of President and Vice-President.* The original method of using electors to choose the President and Vice-President was awkward. Each elector was to vote for two candidates. Then all of the votes were counted. The candidate with the most votes became President, and the runner-up became Vice-President. If no candidate received a majority, the House of Representatives picked the President, and the Senate picked the Vice-President.

In actual practice the process did not work very well. In 1800, a dispute arose when Thomas Jefferson and Aaron Burr won an equal number of electors. Finally, the tie was broken and Jefferson became President. As soon as the election was decided, an amendment was introduced to solve the problem. In 1804, **Amendment 12** changed the method of picking the executive.

Today, there are separate ballots for President and Vice-President. Electors vote first for the presidential candidates and then hold a separate vote for the vice-presidential candidates.

Over the last two hundred years Congress has received many proposals to alter or abolish the Electoral College. Although it has caused problems, the Electoral College remains an important part of the way we elect the President and Vice-President.

ADDITIONAL MATERIALS U.S. Presidents, their terms, and other statistics can be found on the chart "Presidents of the United States" on pages T18 and T19.

4. *Time of election.* Congress sets a single date when voters across the nation choose the electors. This date is the Tuesday after the first Monday of November. Congress also sets the date when all electors cast their votes for President and Vice-President. This date is in December. Finally, the House of Representatives counts and declares the votes valid during the first week in January following the election.

5. *Qualifications of President.* To be President, a person must have been born a citizen of the United States. Presidents must be at least thirty-five years old and have lived in the United States for at least fourteen years. The qualifications for President are greater than those for the House or Senate.

6. *Vacancy in the office of President.* If death, resignation, impeachment, or other reasons keep the President from carrying out the duties of office, the Vice-President takes over. If both the President and Vice-President are unable to serve, Congress can decide who should serve.

In 1947, Congress amended the Presidential Succession Act of 1886. This act lists who will succeed, or replace, the President. This succession is: 1. Vice-President, 2. Speaker of the House, 3. President *pro tempore* of the Senate, 4. Secretary of State, and 5. the other members of the President's cabinet in an order defined by the act. **Amendment 25,** passed in 1967, sets up procedures for filling vacancies in the vice-presidency and for dealing with disabled but living Presidents.

7. *Salary.* During the constitutional debate, some argued that the President should receive no salary. Only the President's expenses should be paid, they thought. Otherwise, money might corrupt the President. The majority were convinced, however, that without a salary, only the wealthy would run for public office. The salary cannot be changed during a President's term. Nor can the President accept any other salary while serving in office.

Today, Congress has set the President's salary at $400,000 per year, with a $50,000 expense account. The President is also given money for travel and official entertaining. The Vice-President receives $181,400 per year, and $10,000 for expenses.

Presidents receive other benefits to help carry out official duties. Specially equipped planes and cars are always ready, free of charge. They live in the White House, with a staff of nearly one hundred servants. When Presidents retire, they get a lifetime pension.

4. The Congress may determine the time of choosing the electors, and the day on which they shall give their votes; which day shall be the same throughout the United States.

5. No person except a natural-born citizen, or a citizen of the United States, at the time of the adoption of this Constitution, shall be eligible to the office of President; neither shall any person be eligible to that office who shall not have attained to the age of thirty-five years, and been fourteen years a resident within the United States.

6. In case of the removal of the President from office, or of his death, resignation, or inability to discharge the powers and duties of the said office, the same shall devolve on the Vice President, and the Congress may by law provide for the case of removal, death, resignation or inability, both of the President and Vice President, declaring what officer shall then act as President, and such officer shall act accordingly, until the disability be removed, or a President shall be elected.

7. The President shall, at stated times, receive for his services, a compensation, which shall neither be increased nor diminished during the period for which he shall have been elected, and he shall not receive within that period any other emolument from the United States, or any of them.

8. Before he enter on the execution of his office, he shall take the following oath or affirmation:—"I do solemnly swear (or affirm) that I will faithfully execute the office of President of the United States, and will to the best of my ability, preserve, protect and defend the Constitution of the United States."

SECTION 2

1. The President shall be commander in chief of the Army and Navy of the United States, and of the militia of the several states, when called into the actual service of the United States; he may require the opinion, in writing, of the principal officer in each of the executive departments, upon any subject relating to the duties of their respective offices, and he shall have the power to grant reprieves and pardons for offenses against the United States, except in cases of impeachment.

8. *Oath of office for the President.* Before taking office, the President must take an oath to support the Constitution and faithfully carry out the duties of office.

SECTION 2: Powers of the President

At first glance, the powers listed here seem rather limited. But in reality the President's power and influence are enormous. Besides the listed powers, Congress has given the President emergency powers to deal with wars or economic depressions. At other times, Presidents have claimed powers not given specifically to Congress or the judicial branch. As leader of his or her political party, the President also has many allies willing to work and vote for his or her proposals. In addition, the President, as the nation's leader, can rally the American people behind certain causes.

1. *Commander in chief, cabinet, and pardons.* Because they wanted the military to be controlled by civilians, the framers made the President **commander in chief** of the armed forces and of any state militia called to serve the United States.

When making decisions, the President may ask for advice from the department heads within the executive branch. Together these department heads make up the President's cabinet. Although the Constitution does not mention a presidential cabinet or cabinet meetings, this clause implies they can exist.

The President can grant reprieves, or delays of punishment, and forgive crimes against the United States, except for cases of impeachment.

The President lives and works in the White House, Washington, D.C.

ADDITIONAL MATERIALS The departments of the executive branch are listed in "The Executive Branch" on page T16.

26

ADDITIONAL MATERIALS For further explanation of the President's cabinet, see Chart 5, "Functions of the Executive Department" on page T17.

2. *Treaties and appointments.* The President can make treaties, or agreements with other countries. All treaties must be approved by two-thirds of the Senate. The President can also appoint members of the cabinet, ambassadors, Supreme Court justices, and other federal officials. These appointments also need the Senate's approval.

This clause shows another instance of "checks and balances" in the Constitution. The President sets overall foreign policy, but the Senate can check the President's power by disapproving a treaty. The Senate can also disapprove a presidential appointment.

Congress can, however, pass laws giving the President and department heads power to appoint less important officials without congressional approval. This simplifies the day-to-day working of government.

3. *Filling temporary vacancies in offices.* If a vacancy occurs when the Senate is *not* in session, the President can grant appointments to temporarily fill the office. When the next Senate session ends, so does the temporary appointment.

SECTION 3: Duties of the President

The President must report the nation's condition to Congress. The President usually does this in a State of the Union speech before a joint session of the House and Senate in January. The President often uses this speech to propose laws. This is one of the ways the framers involved the President in lawmaking.

The President can also call special sessions of Congress, such as the joint session for delivering the State of the Union speech. The President can also adjourn Congress in special situations, but this has never happened.

As official host of the United States, the President welcomes ambassadors and other important officials from foreign nations. As chief executive, the President is responsible for making sure that all federal laws are carried out. The President also signs the papers giving federal officers the authority to act.

SECTION 4: Impeachment of Federal Officers

The President, Vice-President, and other civil officials can be impeached by the House of Representatives. The Senate then acts as a court to decide if the accused official is guilty. If found guilty, the official will be removed from office. Reread Article I, Section 2, Clause 5, and Section 3, Clauses 6 to 7 to review Congress's role in impeachment. To avoid impeachment, President Nixon resigned in 1974. To find out more, read the case study, *"U.S. v. Nixon."*

2. He shall have power, by and with the advice and consent of the Senate, to make treaties, provided two-thirds of the senators present concur; and he shall nominate, and by and with the advice and consent of the Senate, shall appoint ambassadors, other public ministers and consuls, judges of the Supreme Court, and all other officers of the United States, whose appointments are not herein otherwise provided for, and which shall be established by law: but the Congress may by law vest the appointment of such inferior officers, as they think proper, in the President alone, in the courts of law, or in the heads of departments.

3. The President shall have power to fill up all vacancies that may happen during the recess of the Senate, by granting commissions which shall expire at the end of their next session.

SECTION 3

He shall from time to time give to the Congress information of the state of the Union, and recommend to their consideration such measures as he shall judge necessary and expedient; he may, on extraordinary occasions, convene both houses, or either of them, and in case of disagreement between them, with respect to the time of adjournment, he may adjourn them to such time as he shall think proper; he shall receive ambassadors and other public ministers; he shall take care that the laws be faithfully executed, and shall commission all the officers of the United States.

SECTION 4

The President, Vice President and all civil officers of the United States, shall be removed from office on impeachment for, and conviction of, treason, bribery, or other high crimes and misdemeanors.

Case Study: *United States v. Nixon*

". . . it is . . . the duty of the judicial department to say what the law is."
—Majority Opinion, *United States v. Nixon,* 1974

President Richard M. Nixon had a commanding lead during the 1972 election over his Democrat challenger. Then on the evening of June 17, Washington, D.C. police answered a burglar alarm at the Watergate office complex. There they arrested seven men hiding electronic spying equipment in the Democratic Party's national headquarters. Some of the suspects, police found, worked for the Republican Committee to Re-Elect the President. Although Republican officials and the President quickly denied knowledge of the break-in, many people felt the President was trying to create a cover-up.

As the investigation continued, evidence of more serious crimes began to come out. On April 20, 1973, three of the President's close advisors resigned. Other individuals faced criminal charges.

Then in 1974 investigators discovered the President had tape recorded all conversations in his office since 1971. Investigators quickly asked the President to turn over tapes for the time just before and after the break-in. Nixon refused. Because of "executive privilege," he felt he did not have to reveal conversations with his advisors. This privilege, the President argued, was important to the separation of powers.

Finally, the question reached the Supreme Court. Did a President have the right to withhold this information? On July 24, 1974, the Supreme Court ruled no, by a vote of 8–0. Although "executive privilege" is an important safeguard, it is not unconditional. In this case, "executive privilege" was being used to hinder a criminal investigation. The President had to turn over the tapes.

From the tapes, it was clear the President had been part of a cover-up. As the House pondered impeachment proceedings, Richard M. Nixon resigned. In the end, the basic concept of constitutional government—rule by the law— won out.

The idea of executive privilege was tested during the Watergate investigations when Nixon withheld taped conversations containing evidence of a crime. A Supreme Court decision ruled that Nixon had to turn over the tapes.

REVIEW

1. Why is the concept of "executive privilege" important?

2. Why did President Nixon have to resign from office after releasing the tapes?

3. Can you imagine other events that might cause a President to resign from office? Give examples.

REVIEW ANSWERS   1. It's an important factor in the "separation of powers."   2. He faced impeachment and possible removal from office.   3. Answers will vary. Students might point out scandal involvement, criminal activity, or inability to carry out duties.

28

LESSON 5
The Court System

The framers, many of them lawyers themselves, had a special interest in and respect for the law, especially the English system of common law. English **common law** is based on two important ideas. The first is that every person's rights and liberties deserve legal protection. The second is the idea that judges' decisions can have as much weight as laws passed by Congress. These decisions are based on social customs, past rulings in similar cases, and the judge's ideas about the meaning of laws. In **Article III,** the framers created a judicial branch that reflects both these ideas.

Section 1 creates the Supreme Court and gives Congress the power to create other federal courts. **Section 2** describes the judicial branch's power and guarantees the right to a jury trial. **Section 3** deals with the special crime of treason. As the third side of the federal triangle, the framers hoped, the judicial branch would "balance and check" the power of Congress and the President. Today, through custom and practice, these hopes have been fulfilled.

 ARTICLE III

SECTION 1: The Judicial Branch

Because the Articles of Confederation were basically concerned with states' rights, they did not create a national system of courts. Instead, legal cases were tried in state courts. Congress could only appoint special courts to deal with disputes between states.

Delegates at Philadelphia soon agreed that a national judiciary or court system was needed. Article III created a supreme national court, with the power to make final judgments on all cases it considered. Congress has the power to establish **inferior courts,** courts that have less power than the Supreme Court.

In 1789, Congress passed the **Judiciary Act,** creating a system of federal courts below the Supreme Court. Each state has at least one **U.S. District Court.** If someone wants to challenge a District Court ruling, they can turn to one of thirteen **U.S. Courts of Appeals** before they approach the Supreme Court. In addition, Congress has created other courts.

Federal judges are appointed for life and can only be removed by their death, resignation, or impeachment. In addition, the salary of federal judges cannot be reduced during their time in office. The goal here was to free judges to make their best decisions, without worrying that they might be punished for making unpopular decisions.

SECTION 1

The judicial power of the United States, shall be vested in one Supreme Court, and in such inferior courts as the Congress may from time to time ordain and establish. The judges, both of the Supreme and inferior courts, shall hold their offices during good behavior, and shall, at stated times, receive for their services, a compensation, which shall not be diminished during their continuance in office.

OBJECTIVES The student should be able to: **1.** Recognize the importance of the Supreme Court in relation to the other federal courts. **2.** Specify the jurisdiction of the federal courts.　**3.** Analyze the importance of a jury trial.　**4.** Discuss treason and how it is tried and punished.　**5.** Know how justices are appointed to the Supreme Court.

29

SECTION 2

1. The judicial power shall extend to all cases, in law and equity, arising under this Constitution, the laws of the United States, and treaties made, or which shall be made, under their authority;—to all cases affecting ambassadors, other public ministers and consuls;—to all cases of admiralty and maritime jurisdiction;—to controversies to which the United States shall be a party;—to controversies between two or more states;—between a state and citizens of another state;—between citizens of different states,—between citizens of the same state claiming lands under grants of different states, and between a state, or the citizens thereof, and foreign states, citizens or subjects.

2. In all cases affecting ambassadors, other public ministers and consuls, and those in which a state shall be party, the Supreme Court shall have original jurisdiction. In all other cases before mentioned, the Supreme Court shall have appellate jurisdiction, both as to law and fact, with such exceptions, and under such regulations as the Congress shall make.

SECTION 2: Authority of the Federal Courts

1. *Judicial power.* Federal courts have the jurisdiction, or authority, to hear cases that involve the Constitution, federal laws, or any agreements made by the federal government, such as treaties. Federal courts also hear cases that involve ambassadors, shipping, or disputes between different states. Suits brought by citizens or states against another country are also heard by federal courts. **Amendment 11** struck down the provision that federal courts would deal with suits between states or citizens against another state.

2. *The Supreme Court.* If a court has **original jurisdiction,** it is the first court to hear a case. The Supreme Court only has original jurisdiction for cases involving foreign diplomats or a state. Most Supreme Court cases, though, involve the appeal, or review, of decisions made by lower courts. In reviewing a decision, the Supreme Court justices go back over the facts of the case and decide what the law means. They then vote to either uphold or reverse the decision of the lower courts.

This process, called **judicial review,** lets federal courts decide whether court decisions and, more importantly, laws are in keeping with the basic intent of the Constitution. If not, the courts can declare the law **void,** or no longer in effect.

The Constitution does not specifically mention judicial review. In the debates for ratification, however, supporters argued that such a review would be important to any system of checks and balances. In the last 200 years, only a few federal laws have been declared unconstitutional, but over a thousand state and local laws have been declared void.

The nine justices of the Supreme Court review decisions of other courts through the process of judicial review.

POLITICAL SCIENCE According to the system of checks and balances, the Supreme Court has the power to declare laws unconstitutional, but it must rely on the executive branch to enforce its decisions.

3. *Trial by jury.* Any person accused of a crime must be offered a jury trial. If the crime is supposed to have been committed in a specific state, the trial will be held there. If the crime occurred in more than one state or in a territory, Congress can pass laws to say where such trials will be held. The only exception are impeachments, which are tried by the Senate.

This clause did not satisfy the opponents of the Constitution. Although it seems clear enough today, in practice it did not cover some cases. When the Bill of Rights was introduced, the Anti-Federalists insisted that the right to trial be made more specific. **Amendments 6** and **7** do this.

SECTION 3: Treason

1. *Definition.* Before the Revolution, the framers had seen the English use charges of treason to benefit the Crown. Many countries, they knew, commonly defined treason as anything *said* against the government. Because they wanted citizens to be free to question their government, the framers were careful to define **treason** as only making war against the United States or helping its enemies. Some constitutional opponents thought this protection did not go far enough, though. The result was the **First Amendment** protection of free speech.

The framers were also concerned that individuals might be falsely accused of treason. Thus, they added safeguards concerning the evidence needed to convict someone of treason. The testimony of one person is not enough, since that person might be acting out of spite. Either the suspect must confess in court or two people must testify they witnessed the same act of treason.

The first treason case under the Constitution was tried in 1806. The case, argued before the Supreme Court, allowed the Court to interpret the Constitution's definition of treason.

2. *Punishment for treason.* Congress can set the punishment for someone convicted of treason. In 1790, for example, Congress passed a law saying the punishment for treason would be death. Then, in 1861, the Civil War broke out. Millions of Southerners were openly levying war against the United States. To punish so many acts of treason by death was clearly impractical and harmful to the nation's survival. Congress then passed new laws to impose fines and prison terms for traitors during civil insurrections. This shows how the general wording of the Constitution allows the nation's leaders to adapt to changing circumstances.

In other countries, a conviction for treason was said to "corrupt the blood," meaning that the traitor's family and future generations could also be punished. Under the Constitution, only the traitor can be punished and forced to give up honors, military awards, and possessions received as payment for spying.

3. The trial of all crimes, except in cases of impeachment, shall be by jury; and such trial shall be held in the state where the said crimes shall have been committed; but when not committed within any state, the trial shall be at such place or places as the Congress may by law have directed.

SECTION 3

1. Treason against the United States, shall consist only in levying war against them, or in adhering to their enemies, giving them aid and comfort. No person shall be convicted of treason unless on the testimony of two witnesses to the same overt act, or on confession in open court.

2. The Congress shall have power to declare the punishment of treason, but no attainder of treason shall work corruption of blood, or forfeiture except during the life of the person attained.

Profile: "The Great Chief Justice"

Chief Justice John Marshall helped establish the principle of judicial review with his decision in Marbury v. Madison.

"The government of the Union is . . . a government of the people. Its powers are granted by them, and are to be exercised directly on them, and for their benefit."
—Excerpt from *McCulloch v. Maryland,* 1819

The year was 1803. Both the Constitution and the federal government it created faced many questions. Should the judicial branch be as strong as the other branches? If not, could the federal system survive? In *Marbury v. Madison,* John Marshall, Chief Justice of the Supreme Court, gave his answers.

These were the facts of the case. Outgoing President John Adams had appointed William Marbury a judge. When James Madison, the new Secretary of State, refused to honor Marbury's appointment, Marbury sued in the Supreme Court. The Judiciary Act, he said, gave the Court authority in such matters.

The Court disagreed. The Constitution, the supreme law of the land, Marshall ruled, did *not* give the Court authority here. In addition, that part of the Judiciary Act that said the Court had this power was unconstitutional and void. This case established the principle of judicial review.

During his thirty-four years as Chief Justice, Marshall presided over forty-four constitutional questions. In each case, judicial review preserved and strengthened the central government. In *McCulloch v. Maryland* (1819), for example, Marshall supported the doctrine of **implied powers.** This means that the Constitution implies the federal government has certain powers, even though they are not spelled out. Thus, the power to coin money implied that Congress could set up national banks. States could not tax these banks.

The doctrine of implied powers also played a role in *Gibbons v. Ogden* (1824), which boosted Congress's power to regulate interstate commerce. In both *Fletcher v. Peck* (1810) and *Dartmouth College v. Woodward* (1819), the Court confirmed that states could not interfere with private contracts. These decisions helped create a unified economy.

Marshall was often controversial. When he died in 1836, though, he had earned the recognition that remains his today. Then, as now, he was called the "Great Chief Justice."

REVIEW

1. Why was *Marbury v. Madison* important?

2. Why was Marshall's desire to strengthen the federal government so important during the early years of the nation?

3. Explain why you think Marshall is described as the "Great Chief Justice."

Name _____

REVIEW 2
Lessons 4–5

A. VOCABULARY—ARTICLES II AND III

In the space after each question, write the correct word or phrase *and*
where it is found in the Constitution.

1. This title means the President is in charge of the armed forces and any state militia called to serve the United States. Commander in chief, Art. II, Sec. 2, Cl. 1

2. The Supreme Court is at the head of this branch. Judicial, Art. III, Sec. 1

3. Americans who just criticize their government are not guilty of this crime.
   Treason, Art. III, Sec. 3, Cl. 1

4. This is the highest court in the nation. Supreme Court, Art. III, Sec. 1

5. The leader of this branch is the President. Executive, Art. II, Sec. 1, Cl. 1

6. This term means that a law declared unconstitutional by the Supreme Court is no longer in effect. Void, Art. III, Sec. 2, Cl. 2

7. The Constitution uses this word to describe courts that have less power than the Supreme Court. Inferior, Art. III, Sec. 1

8. If either party in a federal court case wants to challenge a District Court ruling, he or she can then turn to this court. U.S. Court of Appeals, Art. III, Sec. 1

9. The first court to hear a case is said to have this power. Original jurisdiction, Art. III, Sec. 2, Cl. 2

10. This process lets the Supreme Court decide whether lower court decisions and laws are in keeping with the intent of the Constitution. Judicial review, Art. III, Sec. 2, Cl. 2

11. These citizens cast the actual ballots for President. Electors, Art. II, Sec. 1, Cl. 2

12. Congress passed this law to create a system of federal courts below the Supreme Court.
    Judiciary Act, Art. III, Sec. 1

13. Under this proposal, a national court would only deal with federal matters or have power over state courts. New Jersey Plan, Art. III, Sec. 1

B. CRITICAL THINKING

1. Why is it important that Supreme Court justices are appointed to their positions for life? Explain how Presidential appointments of justices can affect decisions made by the Court.
   They can make their judgments without fear of punishment for

   unpopular decisions. Presidents usually choose individuals

   holding similar political views.

2. Explain how the "balance of powers" is similar to "checks and balances."
   Answers will vary. Possible response: The idea of balance of powers
   is that each branch of government has somewhat equal power. Checks
   and balances are ways that one branch of government can overturn
   what another branch has done. Both balance of powers and checks and
   balances are meant to keep any single branch of government from
   becoming too powerful.

C. FACTS AND IDEAS

On the line to the left of each term or power, write the letter that corresponds to the correct section or clause of Articles II or III.

TERM OR POWER

B   1. Electors cast votes for President and Vice-President.

L   2. Federal courts deal with cases involving the Constitution.

N   3. A trial by jury is guaranteed.

D   4. A President must be at least 35 years old when elected.

E   5. If the President cannot serve, the Vice-President takes over.

G   6. The powers of the President are listed here.

M   7. The Supreme Court has original jurisdiction in some cases.

H   8. The President can make treaties with Congress's consent.

I   9. The President must give the state of the union address to Congress.

C   10. Congress sets the day when electors cast their votes.

J   11. The President may be impeached for wrongdoings.

F   12. The President must swear to uphold the Constitution.

K   13. Federal judges are appointed for life.

O   14. Treason is defined here.

A   15. A President is elected to four-year terms of office.

ARTICLE/SECTION/CLAUSE

A. Art. II, Sec. 1, Cl. 1
B. Art. II, Sec. 1, Cl. 2
C. Art. II, Sec. 1, Cl. 4
D. Art. II, Sec. 1, Cl. 5
E. Art. II, Sec. 1, Cl. 6
F. Art. II, Sec. 1, Cl. 8
G. Art. II, Sec. 2, Cl. 1
H. Art. II, Sec. 2, Cl. 2
I. Art. II, Sec. 3
J. Art. II, Sec. 4
K. Art. III, Sec. 1
L. Art. III, Sec. 2, Cl. 1
M. Art. III, Sec. 2, Cl. 2
N. Art. III, Sec. 2, Cl. 3
O. Art. III, Sec. 3, Cl. 1

★ ★ ★ ★ LESSON 6 ★ ★ ★ ★
Putting the Constitution to Work

The Articles of Confederation had concentrated power in the hands of the states. The Constitution reversed this by concentrating power at the federal level. If the new system was to be accepted, the states needed to know their rights and the rights of their citizens would be protected. **Article IV** provides these guarantees. Realizing they may have forgotten something or that events would make changes necessary, the framers provided a way to change the Constitution in **Article V.** **Article VI** establishes the Constitution as the supreme law over individuals and states. Finally, **Article VII** provides a system for ratifying the Constitution.

 # ARTICLE IV

SECTION 1: Relations among the States

Under the Articles of Confederation, states acted as rivals, not partners in forming a new nation. States bickered over boundaries, feuded over waterways, and ignored contracts and legal notices from other states. To preserve harmony among the states, the framers decided, each state must honor the court decisions, laws, and licenses issued by other states. If needed, Congress can pass laws upholding this section.

SECTION 1

Full faith and credit shall be given in each state to the public acts, records, and judicial proceedings of every other state. And the Congress may by general laws prescribe the manner in which such acts, records, and proceedings shall be proved, and the effect thereof.

SECTION 2: Rights of Citizens

1. *Privileges.* Each state must give citizens from other states the same rights as their own citizens. A Californian visiting Texas, for example, is entitled to the same rights as Texans, but the Californian must obey Texas laws while visiting Texas. There are only a few exceptions. Visitors to a state, for instance, cannot vote in state elections.

SECTION 2

1. The citizens of each state shall be entitled to all privileges and immunities of citizens in the several states.

2. *Extradition.* Under the Articles of Confederation, suspected criminals often escaped justice by fleeing across state borders. Now, under this clause, one state governor can ask another state governor to help capture and return the suspect for trial. This process, called **extradition,** helps states maintain law and order.

2. A person charged in any state with treason, felony, or other crime, who shall flee from justice, and be found in another state, shall on demand of the executive authority of the state from which he fled, be delivered up, to be removed to the state having jurisdiction of the crime.

3. No person held to service or labor in one state, under the laws thereof, escaping into another, shall, on consequence of any law or regulation therein, be discharged from such service or labor, but shall be delivered upon claim of the party to whom such service or labor may be due.

SECTION 3

1. New states may be admitted by the Congress into this Union; but no new state shall be formed or erected within the jurisdiction of any other state; nor any state shall be formed by the junction of two or more states, or parts of states, without the consent of the legislatures of the states concerned as well as of the Congress.

2. The Congress shall have power to dispose of and make all needful rules and regulations respecting the territory or other property belonging to the United States; and nothing in this Constitution shall be so construed as to prejudice any claims of the United States, or of any particular state.

3. *Return of runaways.* This clause was a compromise to win the support of the South. Although many framers opposed slavery, the South insisted that the Constitution order the return of runaways. This compromise avoided a showdown over slavery, but the problem did not go away.

Congress once again tried to solve the problem of runaways when it passed the **Compromise of 1850.** One part of this compromise, the **Fugitive Slave Law,** made people in the North mad. It set harsh punishments for anyone helping runaways. When the law was finally challenged in court, it was held to be constitutional under this clause.

Some historians blame the framers for the Civil War. If they had not compromised over slavery in the Constitution, the argument goes, the Civil War would not have occurred. Other historians hold that the compromises were essential. By the time war broke out, the nation was strong enough to survive.

SECTION 3: New States and Territories

1. *Admitting new states.* In 1787, several seaboard states controlled huge tracts of land west to the Mississippi River. Yet, population in these territories was growing so quickly that many were talking about dividing the territories into new states.

This presented a dilemma to the framers. Some feared that new and larger states might have more representatives in Congress than older states. To prevent this, one proposal even suggested limited representation for new states. Instead, the Constitution left admission of new states up to future Congresses. The only restriction was that new states could not be created by dividing or joining already existing states, unless Congress and the state legislatures agreed.

2. *Congressional powers over federal lands.* Congress can sell or give away federal lands and make laws for their government. This clause reflects the success of the **Northwest Ordinance,** one of the last acts passed by the Confederation. This law divided the land north and west of the Ohio River into smaller territories, each governed by officials appointed by Congress. When the population reached 5,000 adult males, the territory could elect its own legislature. When the territory had a population of 60,000, it could apply for statehood. This law set the pattern for the orderly settlement and admission of new states.

Not all settlement went as smoothly. South of the Ohio River, there were no guidelines for settlers. Many settlers claimed they had a right to the same land. Too often, they sued in court. To protect federal and state land claims, the framers added another statement here. Nothing in the Constitution can be seen as prejudicing, or weakening, any federal or state land claim.

SECTION 4: State Guarantees and Protections

The federal government will be sure that every state has a **republican government,** in which people are governed by elected representatives. The federal government will also protect states from invasion. If the state governor asks for help, the federal government will also help a state put down a riot or rebellion.

SECTION 4

The United States shall guarantee to every state in this union a republican form of government, and shall protect each of them against invasion; and on application of the legislature, or of the executive (when the legislature cannot be convened) against domestic violence.

The Fugitive Slave Law set harsh punishments for people helping runaways. Nevertheless, many Northerners did help enslaved people run away. More than 2,000 runaways were hidden in this house in Newport, Indiana, as they escaped to freedom.

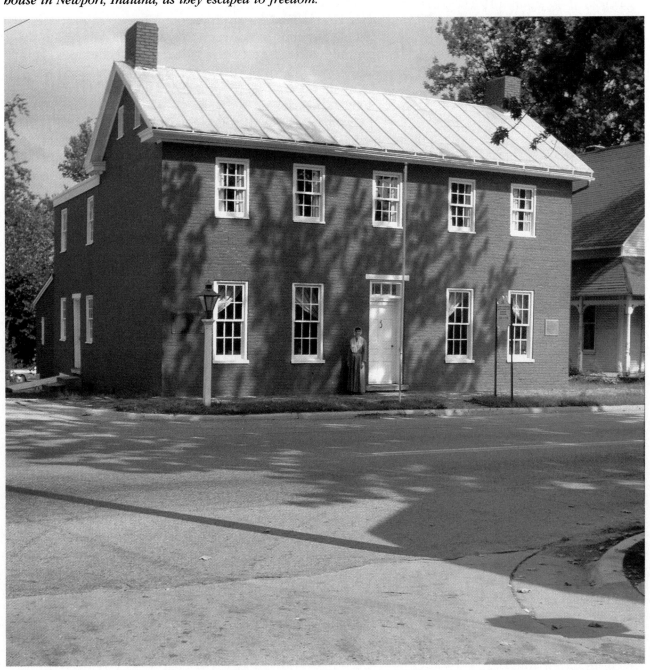

CURRENT EVENTS Discuss with students how the federal government aids states in the event of such natural disasters as hurricanes, floods, or droughts.

ARTICLE V
Amending the Constitution

The Congress, whenever two-thirds of both houses shall deem it necessary, shall propose amendments to this Constitution, or, on the application of the legislatures of two-thirds of the several states, shall call a convention for proposing amendments, which, in either case, shall be valid to all intents and purposes, as part of this Constitution, when ratified by the legislatures of three-fourths of the several states, or by conventions in three-fourths thereof, as the one or the other mode of ratification may be proposed by the Congress; provided that no amendment which may be made prior to the year one thousand eight hundred and eight shall in any manner affect the first and fourth clauses in the ninth section of the first article; and that no state, without its consent, shall be deprived of its equal suffrage in the Senate.

The Articles of Confederation had been too difficult to amend, or change. Yet, the framers worried, if they made the Constitution too easy to change, it would not be respected. Again, they sought a compromise.

Amendments can be proposed if two-thirds of both the House and Senate approve. As an alternative, two-thirds of the state legislatures can ask Congress to hold a national convention for proposing amendments.

Amendments become a part of the Constitution when they are **ratified,** or approved, by three-fourths of the state legislatures or conventions called for ratification. Beginning with **Amendment 19,** an amendment must be ratified within seven years. An exception was made in 1979. To find out more, read the case study, ''The Equal Rights Amendment.''

As another North-South compromise, no amendment proposed before 1808 could outlaw slavery or change the method of levying taxes. This passage became invalid when **Amendment 13** ended slavery and **Amendment 16** introduced the personal income tax. In addition, no amendment can reduce the number of senators representing a state without the state's consent.

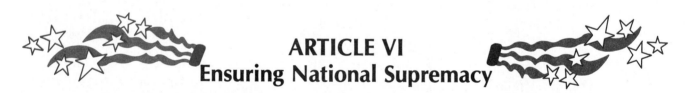

ARTICLE VI
Ensuring National Supremacy

1. All debts contracted and engagements entered into, before the adoption of this Constitution, shall be as valid against the United States under this Constitution, as under the Confederation.

2. This Constitution, and the laws of the United States which shall be made in pursuance thereof; and all treaties made, or which shall be made, under the authority of the United States, shall be supreme law of the land; and the judges in every state shall be bound thereby, anything in the Constitution or laws of any state to the contrary notwithstanding.

1. *Debts owed before the Constitution.* Any national debts that existed before the adoption of the Constitution would be paid by the United States.

2. *Supreme law of the United States.* This was a difficult issue at the convention. Although the Articles of Confederation were supposed to have been the dominant law of the land, states did as they pleased. This weakened the power of the national government. As part of the New Jersey Plan, the phrase ''supreme law'' was suggested to show that the Constitution and acts of Congress were the nation's highest laws. Furthermore, state judges must be sure that no court decision or law conflicts with the Constitution.

POLITICAL SCIENCE The promise of a bill of rights gained the support of Samuel Adams, an Anti-Federalist, who helped sway the vote of Massachusetts in favor of ratification. Many other states also ratified, based on this promise.

38

George Washington swore an oath to defend the Constitution when he became the first President in 1789. Supreme Court Justice Ruth Bader Ginsburg took the same oath.

3. *Oaths to support the Constitution.* Another way to ensure support for the Constitution was to require all office holders to take an oath before assuming office. All executive, legislative, and judicial officials in the federal and state governments must take such an oath. Religion cannot be a qualification for holding public office.

3. The senators and representatives before mentioned, and the members of the several state legislatures, and all executive and judicial officers, both of the United States and of the several states, shall be bound by oath or affirmation, to support this Constitution; but no religious test shall ever be required as qualification to any office or public trust under the United States.

ARTICLE VII
Ratifying the Constitution

Before the Constitution could go into effect, specially called conventions in at least nine states had to ratify it. By submitting the Constitution directly to the states, the framers emphasized their commitment to the republican system they had created. It would be the *people* of the *states* giving their blessings to the *federal* government. A stronger method of approval cannot be imagined. The Constitution of the United States took effect when the ninth state, New Hampshire, ratified it on June 21, 1788.

The ratification of the conventions of nine states, shall be sufficient for the establishment of this Constitution between the states so ratifying the same.

Done in convention by the unanimous consent of the states present the seventeenth day of September in the year of our Lord one thousand seven hundred and eighty-seven and of the independence of the United States of America the twelfth. In witness whereof we have hereunto subscribed our names . . .

ADDITIONAL MATERIALS Use Worksheets 11 and 12 on pages T32 and T33 in conjunction with this lesson.

Case Study: The Equal Rights Amendment

Hundreds of thousands of people rallied to support the Equal Rights Amendment. Nevertheless, the ERA was not ratified, proving that amending the Constitution is very difficult.

"Equality of rights under the law shall not be denied or abridged by the United States or by any state on account of sex."
—From: Section 1, proposed Equal Rights Amendment, 1972

To most of us, seven years seems like a long time. Yet, seven years is not very long where an amendment to the Constitution is concerned. The effort to ratify the Equal Rights Amendment (ERA) is an example.

The amendment was first proposed in 1923, shortly after the Nineteenth Amendment gave women the right to vote. At first, the proposal did not draw wide support. Then in the 1960s, the civil rights movement sparked new interest in women's rights. Led by the **National Organization for Women (NOW),** labor, political, and religious groups pushed to add a guarantee of women's rights to the Constitution.

In 1972, Congress passed the proposed ERA and sent it to the states for ratification. By the end of the year, twenty-two states had ratified ERA. Only fifteen more states needed to ratify ERA before the 1979 deadline.

By 1973, though, organized opposition arose, led by a group called **Stop-ERA.** ERA, they said, threatened women's rights. If ERA passed, Stop-ERA argued, women would be drafted into the military and American family life would be destroyed. Other critics said ERA was not needed, because existing laws protected women's rights.

More states ratified the ERA, but five that had ratified changed their minds. By January 1977, only thirty-five states had ratified ERA. As the 1979 ratification deadline approached, Congress agreed to extend the deadline to June 1982.

For the next three years both sides rallied, debated, and distributed pamphlets. NOW called for an economic boycott of states that had not ratified the ERA. Stop-ERA handed out home-baked bread to emphasize the threat to women in the home. By the June 1982 deadline, though, ERA was still three votes short of ratification. The proposal had failed.

The struggle to ratify ERA shows how difficult it can be to amend the Constitution. It also shows that the democratic process allows citizens the opportunity to propose—and oppose—changes to the government.

REVIEW

1. Why did ERA supporters feel it was needed?

2. Do you think they were correct? Why?

3. In your opinion, is the amending process too difficult? Why?

REVIEW ANSWERS 1. To ensure the rights of women
2. Answers will vary. Students should be able to show support for their opinions. 3. Answers will vary. Students should offer logical support for their opinions.

40

LESSON 7
The Bill of Rights

Critics felt the Constitution was not clear enough in protecting individual rights and liberties. To quiet them, supporters of the Constitution promised to introduce a series of amendments listing these rights. On September 25, 1789, James Madison kept this promise by proposing twelve amendments to the Constitution. The ten amendments that were adopted are known as the **Bill of Rights.**

AMENDMENT 1
Freedom of Religion, Speech, Press; Rights to Assembly and Petition (1791)

This amendment sets out each citizen's basic **civil rights** that are guaranteed by the government. For this reason, the **First Amendment** is perhaps the most important and best-known amendment.

An *established* religion is one the government sets as an official religion. At the time of the Revolution, the Anglican Church was England's official religion. Other religions were not treated fairly. The framers saw people of many different faiths settling in America and believed that religious freedom was a must.

Under British rule, the colonists had experienced both censorship and repression. This convinced them that the Constitution must guarantee both freedom of speech and freedom of the press. People must be free to question the government, express themselves, and exchange information without fear of harm or arrest.

There are some limits, though. Slander, for example, is forbidden. **Slander** is *saying* a lie that is meant to damage another person's reputation. Slander that is *published* is called **libel.** Saying or printing things that would endanger the nation or public is also forbidden. Publishers, for example, cannot print military secrets. People cannot yell "Fire" in a crowded theater simply for the thrill of it.

The right to assembly means that people can hold meetings to discuss public issues. The right to petition government for redress means that the people can ask government to correct a wrongful situation. These rights let citizens influence government peaceably.

> Congress shall make no law respecting an establishment of religion, or prohibiting the free exercise thereof; or abridging the freedom of speech, or of the press; or the right of the people peaceably to assemble, and to petition the government for a redress of grievances.

In the United States, citizens are guaranteed the freedom to worship as they wish by the First Amendment.

OBJECTIVES   The student should be able to: **1.** List the protection given in the Bill of Rights.   **2.** Recognize the necessity for adding the Bill of Rights to the Constitution.   **3.** Explain the importance of Amendment 5, "rights of the accused."   **4.** Understand why Amendment 9 is an added guarantee of the liberties expressed in the Preamble.   **5.** Give examples of Amendment 1 rights.

AMENDMENT 2
Right to Bear Arms (1791)

A well regulated militia, being necessary to the security of a free state, the right of the people to keep and bear arms, shall not be infringed.

The leaders of the states wanted to be able to protect themselves. Thus, private citizens and citizens serving in state militias have a right to be armed.

To some, this means government cannot interfere with gun owners. The courts have generally ruled, though, that government can pass laws to control the possession of weapons. For example, private citizens cannot own some kinds of weapons, such as machine guns. Also, both federal and state laws determine who can be licensed to own firearms. People with criminal records, for example, cannot be licensed to own guns.

AMENDMENT 3
Keeping Troops in Private Homes (1791)

No soldier shall, in time of peace be quartered in any house, without the consent of the owner, nor in time of war, but in a manner to be prescribed by law.

This amendment was meant to prevent the problems that resulted when the British tried to **quarter,** or house, troops in colonists' homes. In national emergencies, though, special laws can be passed to order the temporary housing of troops.

AMENDMENT 4
Search and Seizure (1791)

The right of the people to be secure in their persons, houses, papers, and effects, against unreasonable searches and seizures, shall not be violated, and no warrants shall issue, but upon probable cause supported by oath or affirmation, and particularly describing the place to be searched, and the persons or things to be seized.

Amendments 4 to 8 protect the rights of persons accused of crimes. The American legal system is guided by the idea that each person is "innocent until proven guilty." Thus, government tried to protect the accused person's rights throughout the criminal investigation.

This amendment protects the right to privacy. Law officers must follow strict guidelines before they can violate this privacy. Searches of private homes, for example, must be authorized by a judge, who issues a **search warrant.** To get a search warrant, law officers must show probable cause. **Probable cause** means the search is likely to uncover evidence concerning a crime. The search warrant must be very specific, though, and describe the place to be searched and what is being searched for. The courts have ruled that even illegal items found during an unauthorized search cannot be used as evidence during a trial.

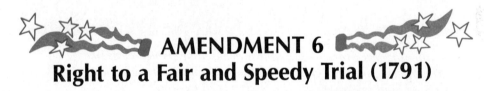

AMENDMENT 5
Rights of Persons Accused of a Crime (1791)

Because of television and movies, taking the "Fifth Amendment," or refusing to testify against yourself, is one of the best-known rights under the Constitution. This is just one of the important protections this amendment provides persons accused of crimes.

No one can be tried for a major crime unless they are indicted, or charged, by a grand jury. A **grand jury** decides if there is good reason to believe the accused person is guilty. The exception is someone who is serving in the military and accused of committing a crime during a military action.

Citizens are also protected from double jeopardy. **Double jeopardy** means a citizen is at risk, or jeopardy, for trial a second time, even if he or she is found innocent in the first trial. Of course, people who are found guilty can appeal, or ask a higher court to decide if there was an error in the first trial.

No one can be imprisoned, executed, or have property taken without due process. **Due process** refers to the guidelines that protect a person's rights during legal proceedings.

Finally, the amendment limits **eminent domain**—the government's power to take private property for public use. If property is needed for a highway, for example, the government must prove it is needed and pay the owner a fair price.

No person shall be held to answer for a capital, or otherwise infamous crime, unless on a presentment or indictment of a grand jury, except in cases arising in the land or naval forces, or in the militia, when in actual service in time of war or public danger; nor shall any person be subject for the same offense to be twice put in jeopardy of life or limb; nor shall be compelled in any criminal case to be a witness against himself, nor be deprived of life, liberty, or property, without due process of law; nor shall private property be taken for public use, without just compensation.

AMENDMENT 6
Right to a Fair and Speedy Trial (1791)

In England, people accused of crimes were held, sometimes for years, without ever standing trial. The right to a "speedy trial" simply means the accused will not have to wait very long before a hearing.

There are also guidelines to ensure the trial is fair. The jury must swear to be objective and fair in weighing the evidence. The accused must be told the exact charges, so that he or she can prepare a proper defense before the trial. The trial itself cannot be secret. It—and the testimony witnesses give—must be public. The accused must be present at the trial and have a chance to question witnesses. The accused can also call witnesses to testify on his or her behalf. Finally, the accused has the right to be represented by a lawyer, even during questioning about a crime.

In all criminal prosecutions, the accused shall enjoy the right to a speedy and public trial, by an impartial jury of the state and district wherein the crime shall have been committed, which district shall have been previously ascertained by law, and to be informed of the nature and cause of the accusation; to be confronted with the witnesses against him; to have compulsory process for obtaining witnesses in his favor, and to have the assistance of counsel for his defense.

CURRENT EVENTS In his film, *The Thin Blue Line,* documentary filmmaker Errol Morris showed what results when evidence is not clearly examined. His investigative efforts, including interviews with witnesses, led to the release of a man whose rights were violated when he was accused of the murder of a Texas policeman.

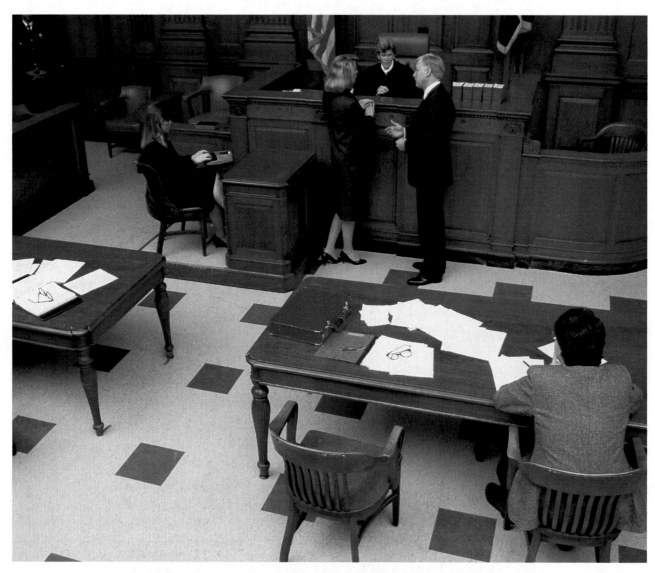

The fifth and sixth amendments protect individuals accused of crimes. Citizens have the right to due process, are protected from double jeopardy, are entitled to fair and speedy trials, and are guaranteed a public trial by jury.

AMENDMENT 7
Trial by Jury in Civil Suits (1791)

In suits at common law, where the value in the controversy shall exceed twenty dollars, the right of trial by jury shall be preserved, and no fact tried by a jury, shall be otherwise reexamined in any court of the United States, than according to the rules of the common law.

Article III and the Sixth Amendment guarantee jury trials for persons accused of crimes. This amendment extends this right to either party in a civil suit involving more than twenty dollars. A civil suit, or case, involves a dispute about individual rights and legal obligations. A dispute about a contract, for example, would be settled by a civil suit.

HISTORY Some of the freedoms listed in the Bill of Rights originated in the English Bill of Rights, passed in 1689, while others were a reaction to British rule.

AMENDMENT 8
Bail and Punishment (1791)

In some cases, the court will decide that an accused person who is awaiting trial can be released from jail if he or she pays bail. **Bail** is a sum of money or property the accused person agrees to give up if he or she fails to return for trial.

Both bail and fines used as punishment must fit the crime. Punishments themselves cannot be cruel or unusual. A shoplifter, for example, cannot be hanged. This amendment has been used to challenge the constitutionality of the death penalty. Beginning in 1972, a series of Supreme Court rulings agreed that the death penalty was "cruel and unusual punishment." Thus, all laws that dealt with the death penalty were void. Then in 1976, a ruling again allowed the death penalty for certain "extreme" crimes, as long as the guidelines for its use were clear. Today, the debate over the death penalty continues.

> Excessive bail shall not be required, nor excessive fines imposed, nor cruel and unusual punishments inflicted.

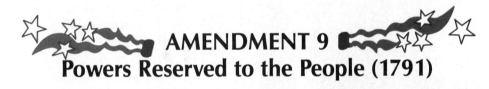

AMENDMENT 9
Powers Reserved to the People (1791)

The framers realized they could not list all the rights of citizens. This amendment was included to make it clear that the "listed" rights were *not* the people's only rights. It satisfied those who worried a bill of rights could be used to limit liberty, not protect it.

> The enumeration in the Constitution, of certain rights, shall not be construed to deny or disparage others retained by the people.

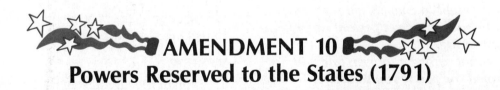

AMENDMENT 10
Powers Reserved to the States (1791)

This amendment aims to make the state's relationship to the federal system clear. All powers that are not specifically given to the federal government or specifically forbidden to the states, are guaranteed to the states or the people.

> The powers not delegated to the United States by the Constitution, nor prohibited by it to the states, are reserved to the states respectively, or to the people.

POLITICAL SCIENCE The rights of citizens of the United States are not absolute. For more than two centuries, the Supreme Court has interpreted the limits and the precise application of these rights.

45

ADDITIONAL MATERIALS Use Worksheets 13 and 14 on pages T34 and T35 in conjunction with this lesson.

Case Study: *Miranda v. Arizona*

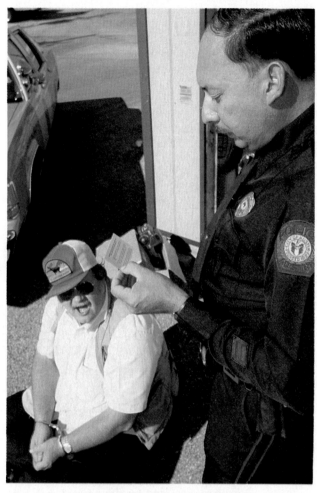

The Miranda decision stated that suspects must be informed of their rights when arrested.

"You have a right to remain silent. Anything you say can and will be used against you in a court of law.
You have a right to consult with a lawyer and to have a lawyer present during any questioning.
If you cannot afford a lawyer, one will be obtained for you if you so desire."
—The Miranda Warning

On March 2, 1963, a young Phoenix, Arizona woman was kidnapped and raped. Two weeks later, police picked up Ernesto Miranda for questioning. At the police station, the victim identified Miranda in a lineup.

For the next two hours, police questioned Miranda in a separate room. Eventually, they convinced him to write down and sign a confession. At the top of the paper was a typed statement saying he understood his rights.

At Miranda's trial, the confession was used as evidence against him. He was convicted and sentenced to prison. The police and court, it seemed, had done a good job. Miranda's court-appointed lawyer was not convinced, however. At no point, he charged, had Miranda been told his Constitutional rights.

The Arizona Supreme Court heard the appeal in 1964. The state court said Miranda knew his rights. Miranda's lawyer appealed the case to the United States Supreme Court.

In 1966 the high court overturned Miranda's conviction by a vote of five to four. Chief Justice Earl Warren wrote the opinion for the majority of justices. Although there was no evidence the police used force to obtain the confession, Miranda had unknowingly testified against himself by signing the confession. This, Warren said, is forbidden by the Fifth Amendment. The Court further agreed that Miranda was not given a chance to consult with a lawyer before or during the questioning. This is guaranteed by the Sixth Amendment. Unless a suspect is clearly told about his or her rights, none of the answers can be used in a trial.

Many felt the Miranda decision favored criminals over the police. However, the major change since the decision is that police are required to tell suspects of their rights. This protects the suspects' rights, and fewer cases are thrown out of court because of police mistakes in dealing with suspects.

REVIEW

1. Explain the circumstances that led to Miranda's conviction.

2. Why is the right to have a lawyer present during questioning important?

3. In your opinion, is the Miranda Warning good or bad? Why?

REVIEW ANSWERS   1. Without a lawyer present, he wrote and signed a confession that also included a statement indicating he understood his rights. This confession was used against him in court.   2. A lawyer can advise his/her client not to answer incriminating questions.   3. Answers will vary. Students should point out that it does protect the rights of suspects.

REVIEW 3
Lessons 6–7

A. VOCABULARY—ARTICLES V–VII AND THE BILL OF RIGHTS

(1) In the space after each question, write the correct word or phrase *and* where it can be found in the Constitution.

1. This term means an amendment has been approved by a state.
   _____ Ratified, Art. V _____

2. A citizen can be tried for the same crime twice. __Double jeopardy, Amendment 5__

3. Iowa agrees to return a suspect to Ohio for trial. __Extradition, Art. IV, Sec. 2, Cl. 2__

4. This is another term for housing troops. __Quarter, Amendment 3__

5. These rights are guaranteed by the government. __Civil rights, Amendment 1__

6. A suspect can pay this to guarantee he or she will return for trial.
   _____ Bail, Amendment 8 _____

7. Slander that is published is called this. __Libel, Amendment 1__

8. The police must show this to obtain a search warrant. __Probable cause, Amendment 4__

9. This group indicts people for major crimes. __Grand jury, Amendment 5__

10. This protects citizens' rights during legal proceedings. __Due process, Amendment 5__

11. This allows police to search private homes. __Search warrant, Amendment 4__

12. This is saying a lie that is meant to harm another person's reputation.
    _____ Slander, Amendment 1 _____

13. The government takes a farm so it can build a highway. __Eminent domain, Amendment 5__

B. CRITICAL THINKING

1. Give three examples from Articles IV, V, or VI that show that the national government has power over the states.

   Answers will vary. Possible answers include: Each state must grant

   rights to citizens of other states; fugitives must be extradited;

   the law of the U.S. was the "supreme law" of the land;

   officeholders had to take an oath to uphold the Constitution before

   assuming office.

   _____

2. Why did the framers think it was necessary to give the national government power over the states?

The Articles of Confederation did not give the national government

enough power, so states did as they wished. This caused confusion

that threatened the future of the country.

_____

_____

C. FACTS AND IDEAS

On the line to the left of each term or power, write the letter that corresponds to the correct portion of Articles IV to VII or the Bill of Rights.

TERM or POWER	ARTICLE/AMENDMENT
T 1. Powers not given the federal government are reserved to the states or the people.	**A.** Art. IV, Sec. 1
B 2. Visitors to a state have the same rights as state citizens.	**B.** Art. IV, Sec. 2, Cl. 1
N 3. Unreasonable searches and seizures are prohibited.	**C.** Art. IV, Sec. 2, Cl. 2
D 4. Congress is given the power to create new states.	**D.** Art. IV, Sec. 3, Cl. 1
K 5. Freedom of the press is guaranteed.	**E.** Art. IV, Sec. 3, Cl. 2
F 6. The federal government will protect states from invasion.	**F.** Art. IV, Sec. 4
G 7. Three-fourths of the states must ratify an amendment.	**G.** Article V
Q 8. Jury trials are guaranteed for civil suits involving more than twenty dollars.	**H.** Art. VI, Sec.2
H 9. The Constitution is the supreme law of the land.	**I.** Art. VI, Sec. 3
R 10. Cruel and unusual punishments are forbidden.	**J.** Article VII
E 11. Congress can sell federal lands.	**K.** Amendment 1
A 12. Each state must honor the laws of the other states.	**L.** Amendment 2
I 13. Federal officials must swear to uphold the Constitution.	**M.** Amendment 3
C 14. Extradition is authorized.	**N.** Amendment 4
P 15. People have the right to confront their accusers.	**O.** Amendment 5
L 16. The right to bear arms is guaranteed.	**P.** Amendment 6
M 17. Quartering troops in private homes is forbidden during peacetime.	**Q.** Amendment 7
O 18. People cannot be forced to testify against themselves.	**R.** Amendment 8
J 19. Nine states needed to ratify the Constitution to make it legal.	**S.** Amendment 9
S 20. The powers listed in the Constitution are not the only rights guaranteed to the people.	**T.** Amendment 10

★ ★ ★ ★ LESSON 8 ★ ★ ★ ★
Nineteenth-Century Amendments

Five amendments were ratified between 1795 and 1870.
Amendment 11 changed the rules for suing states, and **Amendment 12** clarified the way the President and Vice-President are elected. **Amendments 13, 14,** and **15** reflect changes resulting from the Civil War.

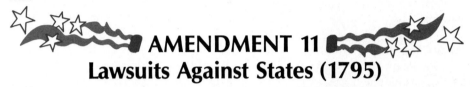

AMENDMENT 11
Lawsuits Against States (1795)

Under Article III, a state could be sued by a citizen from another state. During the debates for ratification, the Anti-Federalists labeled this a threat to state power. The Federalists, though, assured them no state could be sued without its consent. Then in 1793, a man from South Carolina sued the state of Georgia in federal court. The state refused to appear in court, since it had not given consent. The Supreme Court ruled against Georgia.

The next year, this amendment was passed. Federal courts no longer can try cases in which a state is sued by citizens of another state or a foreign country. This is the only amendment to limit the judicial branch.

> The judicial power of the United States shall not be construed to extend to any suit in law or equity, commenced or prosecuted against one of the United States by citizens of another state, or by citizens or subjects of any foreign state.

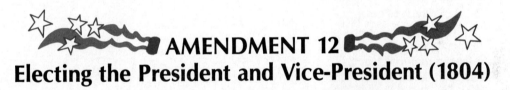

AMENDMENT 12
Electing the President and Vice-President (1804)

This amendment was adopted to clarify and solve some problems with the electoral process established in Article II. (To review the problem, see the discussion of the election of 1800 with Article II, Section 1, Clause 3.) Before this amendment, only one ballot was used when the electors voted for President and Vice-President. The candidate with the most votes became President, and the runner-up became Vice-President.

Now electors meet in their own states and use separate ballots to vote for President and Vice-President. The results are then sent to the President of the Senate, who opens and counts the results at a joint session of Congress. The candidate who receives a majority of the votes for President is elected. If no candidate has a majority, the House picks the President from the three candidates having the most votes. When picking a President in this manner, each state has *one* vote, and two-thirds of the states must vote.

> The electors shall meet in their respective states, and vote by ballot for President and Vice President, one of whom, at least, shall not be an inhabitant of the same state with themselves; they shall name in their ballots the person voted for as President, and in distinct ballots the person voted for as Vice President, and they shall make distinct lists of all persons voted for as President, and of all persons voted for as Vice President, and of the number of votes for each, which lists they shall sign and certify, and transmit sealed to the seat of the government of the United States, directed to the president of the Senate;—the president of the Senate

OBJECTIVES The student should be able to: **1.** Compare Amendment 12 procedures for electing a President to the original system in Article II. **2.** Identify the ''Civil War'' amendments (13, 14, 15). **3.** Discuss the importance of Amendment 13.

49

4. Explain how Amendment 14 clarifies and protects the ''rights of citizens.'' **5.** Recognize why specific penalties were imposed against Confederate officials.

shall, in the presence of the Senate and House of Representatives, open all the certificates and the votes shall then be counted;—the person having the greatest number of votes for President, shall be the President, if such number be a majority of the whole number of electors appointed; and if no person have such majority, then from the persons having the highest numbers not exceeding three on the list of those voted for as President, the House of Representatives shall choose immediately, by ballot, the President. But in choosing the President, the votes shall be taken by states, the representation from each state having one vote; a quorum for this purpose shall consist of a member or members from two-thirds of the states, and a majority of all states shall be necessary to a choice. And if the House of Representatives shall not choose a President whenever the right of choice shall devolve upon them, before the fourth day of March next following, then the Vice President shall act as President, as in the case of the death or other Constitutional disability of the President.—The person having the greatest number of votes as Vice President, shall be the Vice President, if such a number be a majority of the whole number of electors appointed, and if no person have a majority, then from the two highest numbers on the list, the Senate shall choose the Vice President; a quorum for the purpose shall consist of two-thirds of the whole number of senators, and a majority of the whole number shall be necessary to a choice. But no person constitutionally ineligible to the office of President shall be eligible to that of Vice President of the United States.

If no candidate has received a majority by January 20 (this date was changed by Amendment 25), the Vice-President acts as President until a new President is chosen.

The Vice-President is picked using nearly the same process. If there is no candidate with a majority, the Senate picks the Vice-President from the two candidates having the most votes. In this case two-thirds of the senators must vote, and a majority is needed to elect the Vice-President.

A vice-presidential candidate must meet the same qualifications as a presidential candidate, since the Vice-President may someday become President.

The election process is a very important feature of our constitutional democracy.

AMENDMENT 13
Slavery Abolished (1865)

SECTION 1: Slavery prohibited

This is the first of three amendments passed as a direct result of the Civil War. In 1863, President Lincoln's Emancipation Proclamation freed only enslaved persons in the Confederacy. Now this amendment ended slavery in all the remaining states and territories. "Involuntary servitude" used to punish convicted criminals is still allowed, though.

SECTION 2: Enforcement

Congress can pass laws to enforce the amendment and punish violators.

SECTION 1

Neither slavery nor involuntary servitude, except as a punishment for crime whereof the party shall have been duly convicted, shall exist within the United States, or any place subject to their jurisdiction.

SECTION 2

Congress shall have power to enforce this article by appropriate legislation.

AMENDMENT 14
Civil Rights in the States (1868)

SECTION 1: Citizenship

Anyone born or naturalized in the United States is a citizen of both the United States and the state where they live. Under this definition, former enslaved people were clearly full citizens. Thus, no state can pass laws that deprive citizens of rights guaranteed by the Constitution without due process of the law. This amendment, perhaps the most important since the Bill of Rights, has been the basis of many court cases concerning civil rights. For example, this amendment was used to support school desegregation. To find out more, read the case study, "*Brown v. Board of Education of Topeka, Kansas.*"

SECTION 1

All persons born or naturalized in the United States, and subject to the jurisdiction thereof, are citizens of the United States and of the state wherein they reside. No state shall make or enforce any law which shall abridge the privileges or immunities of citizens of the United States; nor shall any state deprive any person of life, liberty, or property, without due process of law; nor deny to any person within its jurisdiction the equal protection of the laws.

HISTORY In 1883 the Supreme Court nullified the Civil Rights Act of 1875, which outlawed discrimination against African Americans using public facilities. According to the Court, this nullification did not violate the Fourteenth Amendment, "Individual invasion of individual rights is not the subject-matter of the amendment." The Court felt it applied only to state action.

SECTION 2

Representatives shall be apportioned among the several states according to their respective numbers, counting the whole number of persons in each state; excluding Indians not taxed. But when the right to vote at any election for the choice of electors for President and Vice President of the United States, representatives in Congress, the executive and judicial officers of a state, or the members of the legislature thereof, is denied to any of the male inhabitants of such state, being twenty-one years of age, and citizens of the United States, or in any way abridged, except for participation in rebellion or other crime, the basis of representation therein shall be reduced in the proportion which the number of such male citizens shall bear to the whole number of male citizens twenty-one years of age in such state.

SECTION 3

No person shall be a senator or representative in Congress, or elector of President and Vice President, or hold any office, civil or military, under the United States, or under any state, who, having previously taken an oath, as a member of Congress, or as an officer of the United States, or as a member of any state legislature, or as an executive or judicial officer of any state, to support the Constitution of the United States, shall have engaged in insurrection or rebellion against the same, or given aid or comfort to the enemies thereof. But Congress may by a vote of two-thirds of each house, remove such disability.

SECTION 4

The validity of the public debt of the United States, authorized by law, including debts incurred for payment of pensions and bounties for services in suppressing insurrection or rebellion, shall not be questioned. But neither the United States nor any state shall assume or pay any debt or obligation incurred in aid of insurrection or rebellion against the United States, or any claim for the loss of emancipation of any slave; but all such debts, obligations, and claims shall be held illegal and void.

SECTION 2: Apportionment for the House of Representatives

Section 2 strikes down the portion of Article I that counted only three-fifths of the enslaved persons when apportioning congressional representation. After Amendment 14 became law, the entire population of a state was counted for purposes of determining representation. Because the authors of this amendment were afraid states might try to keep African American citizens from voting, the amendment also provides specific penalties. If a state denies an eligible citizen the right to vote, then the state's number of representatives in Congress will be reduced. This passage issued a challenge to the South to either cooperate or lose representation in Congress.

SECTION 3: Penalties for Confederate officials

This was aimed specifically at former officials in the rebellious Confederate states. Unless two-thirds of Congress approved it, none of them could hold offices in either the state or federal governments.

SECTION 4: Federal debts

Any debts the United States had during the Civil War would be paid by the government. Any debts that the former Confederate states owed would not be paid, nor would former slaveholders be paid for losing their enslaved people. This clause was included to restore faith in the credit of the federal government and to punish those who had aided the rebellious states.

HISTORY The Fifteenth Amendment and other such legislation of the 1860s and 1870s gave the executive branch a great deal of power to eliminate discrimination. It was not until early 1960 that such constitutional power was exercised.

52

SECTION 5: Enforcement

Congress can pass laws to enforce the amendment.

SECTION 5

The Congress shall have power to enforce, by appropriate legislation, the provisions of this article.

African Americans were given their freedom and the right to vote in amendments 13, 14, and 15. However, the struggle for equal rights has continued for more than 100 years, as shown in this giant March on Washington in 1963.

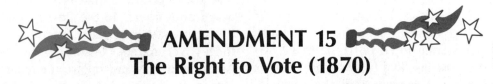

AMENDMENT 15
The Right to Vote (1870)

SECTION 1: Right to vote expanded

This amendment, directed at African Americans, is important for another reason. Before this, the states decided who could vote. Now, for the first time, the federal government acted to protect the right to vote.

Some Southern states refused to cooperate, though. For example, they gave voters **literacy tests.** Whites passed if they could sign their name. African Americans were given difficult readings. If they failed, they were ruled illiterate and ineligible to vote.

SECTION 2: Enforcement

Congress used its power under this section to pass the **Voting Rights Act of 1965.** This gave the federal government the power to supervise state elections and end such unfair practices as literacy tests. As a result, millions of African Americans registered and voted for the first time.

SECTION 1

The right of citizens of the United States to vote shall not be denied or abridged by the United States, or by any state on account of race, color, or previous condition of servitude.

SECTION 2

The Congress shall have power to enforce this article by appropriate legislation.

Case Study: *Brown v. Board of Education of Topeka*

The Supreme Court ruled that separate but equal facilities were unconstitutional in the Brown v. Board of Education of Topeka *decision.*

"In these days, it is doubtful that any child may reasonably be expected to succeed in life if he is denied the opportunity of an education. Such an opportunity, where the state has undertaken to provide it, is a right which must be made available to all on equal terms."
—From opinion in *Brown v. Board of Education of Topeka,* 1954

In 1951, the parents of an eight-year-old African American girl named Linda Brown faced a dilemma. They wanted to enroll Linda in a good school that was just five blocks from their home. School officials, however, said Linda had to attend a school almost two miles away. The closer school was just for whites.

When Linda's parents protested, the school said they were just following a Supreme Court ruling. This ruling, *Plessy v. Ferguson* (1896) had said that separate public facilities for African Americans and white Americans were acceptable as long as they were equal in quality. Since then, the "separate but equal" rule had been used to justify segregated, or separate, schools.

Eventually, the Browns decided to appeal their case to the Supreme Court. Their lawyer was Thurgood Marshall, an African American lawyer for the National Association for the Advancement of Colored People.

The Browns' case rested on the Fourteenth Amendment, which promised all citizens equal rights. Segregated schools did not fulfill that promise, they said. African American schools were not as good as white schools. More importantly, the Browns were able to call on experts who explained that segregated schools made African American children *feel* inferior.

The Court heard and read all the arguments in the case. When Chief Justice Earl Warren read the decision in May 1954, he spoke for a unanimous court. To the Court, education was ". . . the most important function of state and local governments." Although the Fourteenth Amendment did not mention education, it clearly meant that government should extend equal rights and services to all. Thus, the court ruled, "separate educational facilities are inherently unequal."

This ruling began a long, controversial struggle to desegregate the nation's schools. It also strengthened the government's commitment to the civil rights movement.

REVIEW

1. Why were schools segregated before 1954?

2. How does the Fourteenth Amendment show that segregated schools are illegal?

3. How did the *Brown* ruling improve education? Explain your answer.

REVIEW ANSWERS   1. Because of an 1896 Supreme Court ruling, segregated facilities were acceptable if the quality of education was equal.   2. The Fourteenth Amendment provides for equal rights and services for all.   3. Answers will vary. Possible response: it ensured a more free and democratic educational system.

★ ★ ★ ★ LESSON 9 ★ ★ ★ ★

Twentieth-Century Amendments

During the nineteenth century, the Constitution acquired the reputation of being difficult to amend. In our own century, that reputation has not always seemed well deserved. The early years of the twentieth century brought a wave of new amendments—Amendments 16–19—reflecting the political and social concerns of the late Progressive Era. Later, Amendments 23–27 were passed.

AMENDMENT 16
Income Tax (1913)

In 1894 Congress passed a law imposing a tax on income. The Supreme Court found the law unconstitutional, arguing that it violated specific constitutional provisions against certain kinds of taxes. Amendment 16 set aside this ruling and gave Congress authority to levy an income tax.

> The Congress shall have power to lay and collect taxes on incomes, from whatever source derived, without apportionment among the several states, and without regard to any census or enumeration.

AMENDMENT 17
Election of Senators (1913)

Article I, Section 3 originally specified that senators were to be chosen by the legislatures of the states they represented. As a result of Amendment 17, senators are now elected directly by the people. Anyone qualified to vote for members of the lower house in the state legislature can vote for United States senator.

> The Senate of the United States shall be composed of two senators from each state, elected by the people thereof, for six years; and each senator shall have one vote. The electors in each state shall have the qualifications requisite for electors of the most numerous branch of the state legislatures.
>
> When vacancies happen in the representation of any state in the Senate, the executive authority of such state shall issue writs of election to fill such vacancies: **Provided,** That the legislature of any state may empower the executive thereof to make temporary appointments until the people fill the vacancies by election as the legislature may direct.
>
> This amendment shall not be so construed as to affect the election or term of any senator chosen before it becomes valid as part of the Constitution.

OBJECTIVES The student should be able to: **1.** Explain how Amendment 16 changes Article I, Section 9, Clause 4. **2.** Identify the relationship between Amendment 18 and Amendment 21. **3.** Discuss the importance of Amendment 19.

55

4. Recognize how Amendment 24 increased the rights of citizens to vote. **5.** Describe what happens when the President is unable to perform his duties of office.

AMENDMENT 18
Prohibition of Intoxicating Liquors (1919)

SECTION 1
After one year from the ratification of this article the manufacture, sale, or transportation of intoxicating liquors within, the importation thereof into, or the exportation thereof from the United States and all territory subject to the jurisdiction thereof for beverage purposes is hereby prohibited.

SECTION 2
The Congress and the several states shall have concurrent power to enforce this article by appropriate legislation.

SECTION 3
This article shall be inoperative unless it shall have been ratified as an amendment to the Constitution by the legislature of the several states, as provided in the Constitution, within seven years from the date of the submission hereof to the states by the Congress.

The movement to ban alcoholic beverages had been part of American life since the mid-1800s. By 1917 more than half the states had laws against intoxicants, and during World War I, various groups urged that they be banned altogether.

Amendment 18 was passed shortly after the end of the war. It soon proved to be unenforceable. Many objected that the use of alcohol was a private matter and looked for ways around the constitutional ban. The amendment was repealed in 1933 with the passage of Amendment 21.

"I CANNOT TELL A LIE—I DID IT WITH MY LITTLE HATCHET!"
An early prohibition supporter, Carrie Nation, often destroyed barrooms with her hatchet.

AMENDMENT 19
Women's Right to Vote (1920)

The right of citizens of the United States to vote shall not be denied or abridged by the United States or by any states on account of sex.

Congress shall have power to enforce this article by appropriate legislation.

By the early 1900s, several states granted voting rights to women in all elections, at all levels of government. Federal courts, however, had earlier ruled women were not granted the right to vote under any clear provision of the Constitution. To get around this problem, a woman suffrage amendment was introduced to Congress in 1878 and reintroduced every year after that. It was finally passed in 1920 as Amendment 19.

HISTORY Amendment 18 made production of intoxicating liquors a high-volume business. Organized crime prospered and gang-related violence increased until the amendment was repealed in 1933.

HISTORY Even with ratification of Amendment 19, not all women exercised this right. At first, only middle- and upper-class women tended to vote. Today, more women usually vote than men.

AMENDMENT 20
Presidential and Congressional Terms (1933)

SECTION 1: Beginning Terms of Office

Amendment 20 is often called the Lame Duck Amendment, since it dealt with the problem of "lame ducks"—that is, Presidents and members of Congress waiting to leave office after failing reelection or announcing their retirement. Since lame ducks generally represented the policies of the defeated party, they were in a position to affect legislation even though they no longer spoke for the majority of voters. Amendment 20 dealt with this problem by shortening the waiting time between election day and the beginning of a new term.

SECTION 2: Beginning Congressional Sessions

Congressional sessions traditionally began in December, though newly elected members were not seated until March. Section 2 did away with these "lame duck" sessions by making the date of the opening of Congress and the beginning of members' terms the same.

SECTION 3: Presidential Succession

If a President-elect dies before his term begins, or otherwise fails to meet the qualifications for holding office, the Vice-President-elect becomes President.

SECTION 4: Vacancies Filled by Congress

This section specifies the action to be taken by Congress if a candidate for President or Vice-President dies following a presidential election in which no candidate has received a majority of electoral votes.

SECTION 1

The terms of the President and Vice President shall end at noon on the 20th day of January, and the terms of senators and representatives at noon on the third day of January, of the year in which such terms would have ended if this article had not been ratified; and the terms of their successors shall then begin.

SECTION 2

The Congress shall assemble at least once in every year, and such meeting shall begin at noon on the third day of January, unless they shall by law appoint a different day.

SECTION 3

If, at the time fixed for the beginning of the term of the President, the President elect shall have died, the Vice President elect shall become President. If a President shall not have been chosen before the time fixed for the beginning of his term, or if the President elect shall have failed to qualify, then the Vice President elect shall act as President until a President shall have qualified; and the Congress may by law provide for the case wherein neither a President elect nor a Vice President elect shall have qualified, declaring who shall then act as President, or the manner in which one who is to act shall be selected, and such person shall act accordingly until a President or Vice President shall have qualified.

SECTION 4

The Congress may by law provide for the case of the death of any of the persons from whom the House of Representatives may choose a President whenever the right of choice shall have devolved upon them, and for the case of the death of any of the persons from whom the Senate may choose a Vice President whenever the right of choice shall have devolved upon them.

SECTION 5

Sections 1 and 2 shall take effect on the 15th day of October following the ratification of this article.

SECTION 6

This article shall be inoperative unless it shall have been ratified as an amendment to the Constitution by the legislatures of three-fourths of the several states within seven years from the date of its submission.

AMENDMENT 21
Repeal of Prohibition (1933)

SECTION 1

The eighteenth article of amendment to the Constitution of the United States is hereby repealed.

SECTION 2

The transportation or importation into any state, territory, or possession of the United States for delivery or use therein of intoxicating liquors, in violation of the laws thereof, is hereby prohibited.

SECTION 3

This article shall be inoperative unless it shall have been ratified as an amendment to the Constitution by conventions in the several states, as provided in the Constitution, within seven years from the date of the submission hereof to the states by the Congress.

SECTION 1: Repeal

With the failure of prohibition, a variety of plans to repeal or modify Amendment 18 were proposed. The amendment was finally repealed by Amendment 21.

SECTION 2: Prohibition by the States

Individual states could continue to ban alcohol if they so chose. They could also rely on federal support for enforcing state laws against the use and transport of liquor.

AMENDMENT 22
Limit on the Number of Presidential Terms (1951)

SECTION 1

No person shall be elected to the office of the President more than twice, and no person who has held the office of President, or acted as President for more than two years of a term to which some other person was elected President shall be elected to the office of the President more than once. But this article shall not apply to any person holding the office of President when this article was

SECTION 1: Limit on Term of Office

Before Franklin D. Roosevelt, no President had ever served more than two full terms. But Roosevelt's election to third and fourth terms suggested that without constitutional safeguards a President might hold office indefinitely. Amendment 22 limits a President to two full terms in office. It also specifies that no one serving more than two years of another President's term—for example, as Gerald Ford did President Nixon's—can be elected President more than once on his or her own.

HISTORY Although gang violence increased sharply during the years of prohibition, the number of alcoholism-related deaths declined.

58

TEACHING SUGGESTION Have students explain the importance of the Twenty-second Amendment.

Because the Constitution had no limits, Franklin Roosevelt was elected to four terms of office. Amendment 22 limits the number of presidential terms for future presidents to two.

proposed by Congress, and shall not prevent any person who may be holding the office of President, or acting as President, during the term within which this article becomes operative from holding the office of President or acting as President during the remainder of such term.

SECTION 2

This article shall be inoperative unless it shall have been ratified as an amendment to the Constitution by the legislatures of three-fourths of the several states within seven years from the date of its submission to the states by the Congress.

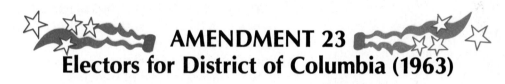

AMENDMENT 23
Electors for District of Columbia (1963)

SECTION 1: Terms of Representation

For many years, the District of Columbia did not take part in presidential elections. The district is not a state within the meaning of the Constitution, and only states could be represented in the Electoral College, where the President is finally chosen. As a result of Amendment 23, district residents now have the right to vote for President, with the district receiving the same number of electors in the Electoral College as the least populous state.

SECTION 1

The district constituting the seat of government of the United States shall appoint in such manner as the Congress may direct:

A number of electors of President and Vice President equal to the whole number of senators and representatives in Congress to which the district would be entitled if it were a state, but in no event more than the least populous state; they shall be in addition to those appointed by the states, but they shall be considered, for the purposes of the election of President and Vice President, to be electors appointed by a state; and they shall meet in the district and perform such duties as provided by the twelfth article of amendment.

SECTION 2

The Congress shall have power to enforce this article by appropriate legislation.

AMENDMENT 24
Poll Taxes (1964)

SECTION 1

The right of citizens of the United States to vote in any primary or other election for President or Vice President, for electors for President or Vice President, or for senator or representative in Congress, shall not be denied or abridged by the United States or any state by reason of failure to pay any poll tax or other tax.

SECTION 2

The Congress shall have power to enforce this article by appropriate legislation.

SECTION 1: Use of Poll Taxes Prohibited

In some southern states as late as the 1960s, poll taxes were used to restrict the rights of poor and African American voters. Amendment 24 prohibited making the payment of such taxes a condition for voting in federal elections.

AMENDMENT 25
Presidential Disability and Succession (1967)

SECTION 1

In case of the removal of the President from office or of his death or resignation, the Vice President shall become President.

SECTION 2

Whenever there is a vacancy in the office of Vice President, the President shall nominate a Vice President who shall take office upon confirmation by a majority vote of both houses of Congress.

SECTION 3

Whenever the President transmits to the president **pro tempore** of the Senate and the speaker of the House of Representatives his written declaration that he is unable to discharge the powers and duties of his office, and until he transmits to them a written declaration to the contrary, such powers and duties shall be discharged by the Vice President as acting President.

SECTION 4

Whenever the Vice President and a majority of either the principal officers of the executive departments or of such other body as Congress may by law provide, transmit to the president **pro tempore** of the Senate and the Speaker of the House of Representatives their written declaration that the President is unable to discharge the powers and duties of his office, the Vice President shall immediately assume the powers and duties of the office as acting President.

SECTION 1: Role of the Vice-President

Article II left unsettled the question of whether a Vice-President actually becomes President or only acts in the President's place if a President dies, resigns, or is removed from office. Amendment 25 specifies that the Vice-President does in fact become President, leaving the office of Vice-President vacant.

SECTION 2: Vice-Presidential Vacancies

Prior to Amendment 25, if the office of Vice-President fell vacant before the end of term, the vacancy was left unfilled. Section 2 establishes constitutional procedures for filling such vacancies if they occur.

SECTION 3: Declaration of Disability

If for any reason the President declares himself or herself unable to perform the duties of his or her office, the Vice-President becomes Acting President, a role formally established by this section of the amendment.

SECTION 4: Disability Not Acknowledged

Section 4 sets up constitutional procedures for dealing with a President who either cannot or will not acknowledge that he is disabled. It also provides for the President's return to office after he has recovered from his disability.

HISTORY In 1919, President Woodrow Wilson suffered a stroke. Wilson's wife at that point carried out many of his presidential tasks. Amendment 25 was designed to prevent another such situation.

While President Reagan recovered from an assassination attempt, Vice-President Bush followed the plan of Amendment 25 and acted as President.

Thereafter, when the President transmits to the president **pro tempore** of the Senate and the Speaker of the House of Representatives his written declaration that no inability exists, he shall resume the powers and duties of his office unless the Vice President and a majority of either the principal officers of the executive departments or of such other body as Congress may by law provide, transmit within four days to the president **pro tempore** of the Senate and the Speaker of the House of Representatives their written declaration that the President is unable to discharge the powers and duties of his office. Thereupon Congress shall decide the issue, assembling within forty-eight hours for that purpose if not in session. If the Congress, within twenty-one days after receipt of the latter written declaration, or, if Congress is not in session, within twenty-one days after Congress is required to assemble, determines by two-thirds vote of both houses that the President is unable to discharge the powers and duties of his office, the Vice President shall continue to discharge the same as acting President; otherwise, the President shall resume the powers and duties of his office.

AMENDMENT 26
Voting Rights for Eighteen-Year-Olds (1971)

SECTION 1: Minimum Age for Voting

In 1970, in response to public pressure, Congress attempted to make eighteen the national minimum voting age. The Supreme Court ruled that Congress was not authorized to set voting-age requirements for the states. Amendment 26 sidestepped the ruling by guaranteeing all citizens eighteen and older the right to vote.

SECTION 1
The right of citizens of the United States, who are eighteen years of age or older, to vote shall not be denied or abridged by the United States or by any state on account of age.
SECTION 2
The Congress shall have power to enforce this article by appropriate legislation.

AMENDMENT 27
Restraint on Congressional Salaries (1992)

No law, varying the compensation for the services of Senators and Representatives, shall take effect, until an election of Representatives shall have intervened.

Any increase in the salaries of members of Congress will take effect in the subsequent session of Congress.

ADDITIONAL MATERIALS Use Worksheets 17 and 18 on pages T38 and T39 in conjunction with this lesson.

61

HISTORY The 27th Amendment was proposed by James Madison in 1789 as part of 12 proposed amendments; 10 of these amendments were ratified in 1791 and are known as the Bill of Rights. The 27th Amendment was not ratified until 1992.

Profile: William O. Douglas

William O. Douglas served on the Supreme Court longer than any other justice. Through thirty-six years on the bench, he acted as the Court's leading spokesman for civil liberties and First Amendment rights.

Douglas was born in Minnesota in 1898, the son of a Presbyterian missionary. His early years were filled with sickness and hardship, but his keen mind won him a scholarship to college. After graduating from law school in 1925, he worked briefly as a Wall Street attorney, but soon became a professor of law.

Douglas soon acquired a reputation as an expert in business and financial law. In 1934 he was assigned to conduct a study on the stock market. His hard work and intelligence won the respect of President Roosevelt.

In 1939, Roosevelt appointed Douglas to the Supreme Court. He soon became known for his aggressive approach to the law. He insisted that living law must be flexible and that the Court should not be bound by old opinions.

But if law was flexible, the values underlying it were not. For Douglas, these fundamental values were to be found in the Bill of Rights. Douglas was an intense defender of the rights of individuals against what he called the "coercive power" of government. In desegregation cases he stood by the principle that all citizens enjoy absolute equality under the Constitution.

Because of his unwavering defense of rights to free expression in First Amendment cases, Douglas was sometimes labeled a dangerous radical. Several times he was threatened with impeachment—once for inciting "violence, anarchy, and civil unrest" in a book he authored.

Douglas was an author, traveler, and conservationist. He never ran for office and twice was considered a serious candidate for Vice-President. In 1975 Douglas retired from the Court, and he died in 1980. He still is widely admired for his firm constitutional commitments and his direct, emotional approach to the law. Judges were not neutral, Douglas believed, and never could be. William O. Douglas gave the law his passion. He also gave it a human face.

Justice William O. Douglas was a strong defender of civil rights and the First Amendment.

REVIEW

1. What did Douglas consider to be more important—protecting individual rights or running the government efficiently?

2. Do you agree with Douglas that judges cannot decide cases without being affected by personal beliefs?

62

★ ★ ★ ★ **LESSON 10** ★ ★ ★ ★

The Living Constitution

For over 200 years the Constitution has been the engine of our national success. It has been a symbol of pride, a force for national unity, and a quiet, steady influence in our daily lives. Sometimes it may even seem *too* quiet, like a "machine that would go of itself," as one nineteenth-century writer put it. The writer feared that we might lose sight of the Constitution and forget that it is there. A constitution that works too well is a mixed blessing. But it's a blessing that many other nations often have wished they had.

The Constitution as a Model

Almost from the time it was written, the United States Constitution has served as a model for others. During the early 1790s, leaders of the French Revolution drew up a constitution borrowing heavily from our own. Later German revolutionaries did much the same in drafting a model constitution for their own experiment in federal unity. Two of England's colonies—Canada and Australia—modeled their constitutions on ours when they became self-governing nations. And many South and Central American countries looked to their northern neighbor for constitutional ideas when they achieved their independence. National interests and traditions undoubtedly played a part in shaping these constitutions, but many of the plans in them—such as separation of powers, two-house legislatures, elected presidents—can be traced to our Constitution.

As the United States grew in power and wealth, many smaller, poorer nations became unwilling to follow our constitutional example. Still, several features of our system continued to appeal to them. The Bill of Rights, with the protection it extends to individual citizens, was widely admired and copied. Some countries even used United States court decisions as models for their own administration of justice.

Constitutional Flexibility

The real test of any constitution is the way it serves its own people. As historical conditions change, so do the needs of a nation. A workable constitution must be able to adjust to these changing needs as they arise, to renew itself without violence and upheaval. Too often in many countries this has not occurred. Constitutional protests have challenged the government and armed conflict has re-

Timeline for Lesson 10

The following Supreme Court decisions were important landmarks in the way that the Constitution was used and interpreted.

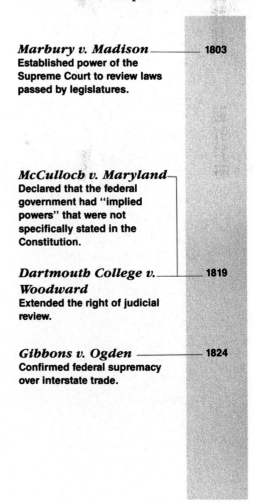

Marbury v. Madison —— 1803
Established power of the Supreme Court to review laws passed by legislatures.

McCulloch v. Maryland
Declared that the federal government had "implied powers" that were not specifically stated in the Constitution.

Dartmouth College v. —— 1819
Woodward
Extended the right of judicial review.

Gibbons v. Ogden —— 1824
Confirmed federal supremacy over interstate trade.

OBJECTIVES The student should be able to: **1.** Recognize why the Constitution has survived intact for over two hundred years. **2.** Explain non-specified governmental powers to intervene. **3.** Discuss some things government has done under the provision of "providing for the general welfare." **4.** Know how the Constitution changes informally. **5.** Analyze the importance of the Constitution's ability to be peacefully changed.

sulted. Protesters have been arrested, kidnapped, sometimes killed. The United States has had its own share of violent incidents—the Civil War was one long, violent argument over how the Constitution should be read and whether it should be changed. But for the most part, change for us has come peacefully, through methods that are part of the constitutional system itself.

The most obvious form of constitutional change is the constitutional amendment. But amending the Constitution was not intended to be easy. The framers did not want a document that was too rigid, but they also did not want one that could be amended too easily. For the most part, constitutional changes have come about not by formal amendment but by informal, everyday adjustment. Changes have come through elections, court decisions, and acts of Congress. Because of this ability to change informally, many people say we have a "living Constitution."

Congress helps our Constitution change and adapt with the legislation it passes. Many congressional actions extend and make parts of the Constitution more clear. For example, Article III specifies that judicial power "shall be vested in one Supreme Court, and in such inferior courts as the Congress may . . . establish." In 1789 Congress passed a law establishing a whole system of *inferior* courts—to fill the gaps in our judicial branch of government. The Constitution did not *require* Congress to act as it did, but Congress acted anyway. Other congressional actions, like civil-rights legislation, have turned unclear areas of constitutional protection into law.

The office of the President has also played a role in keeping the Constitution flexible. For example, the President is bound by Article II to get Senate approval for any treaty he or she concludes. But Presidents can make agreements that are like treaties without Senate approval and without violating the Constitution. Presidents have also made room for themselves in areas normally reserved for Congress. Only Congress has the constitutional power to make laws, but Presidents can issue executive orders—orders with the force of law—in times of emergency or whenever Congress authorizes them to do so.

The courts, too, have helped change the Constitution. Attitudes change, justices come and go, and rulings can be reversed or changed. For example, in the 1890s the Supreme Court ruled that "separate but equal" treatment of different races was constitutionally acceptable. Schools, buses, public rest rooms, and so on could be set aside for whites as long as other *equal* facilities were available for African Americans. But in the 1950s the Supreme Court ruled that such treatment was *not* constitutionally acceptable. Same Constitution, same points of law, but the attitudes of the court—and the country as a whole—had changed. Courts

1857 ———— ***Dred Scott v. Sandford***
Verified that enslaved persons were the property of their owners and could be bought and sold.

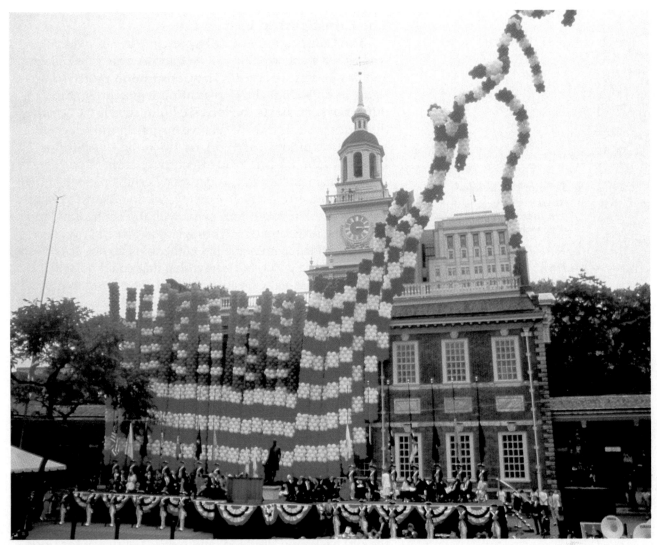

The Bicentennial celebration marked the two hundredth anniversary of the Declaration of Independence. This celebration took place at Freedom Hall in Philadelphia where the Constitution was signed.

do not like to reverse themselves, but reversals are sometimes necessary if the Constitution is to work as it should.

One final source of constitutional change was not anticipated by the framers. The development of political parties—those "warring factions" the framers often warned against—has been a force for constitutional change. Parties provide organization for political and social action and for the expression of ideas on what the Constitution means or ought to mean. They give the average citizen a chance to be heard and to influence the course of government. The wars between parties have meant peaceful change for us, and for the Constitution as well.

Plessy v. Ferguson ———— 1896
Stated that "separate but equal" accommodations for African Americans and whites was legal.

POLITICAL SCIENCE The organization of two political parties began with the formation of local political clubs and the publication of a national political newspaper. The parties first ran in opposition in 1796.

65

The Constitution in Our Lives

The Constitution is a daily presence in our lives. We read as we want, worship as we choose, vote as we like, and criticize as we see fit. The Constitution protects our rights to do so. But the Constitution is also present in other ways. It affects the jobs we hold, the air we breathe, the foods we eat, the TV sets we buy, even though there is no mention of jobs, air, food, or TV in the Constitution. How does the Constitution affect these areas of our lives?

The main answer to this question lies in a passage known as the "commerce clause." Article I, Section 8 gives Congress the power to "regulate commerce with foreign nations, and among the several states." Through more than 150 years of court decisions, commerce has come to mean not just the act of transporting goods but everything that could possibly be affected by that act. Consider a pair of shoes produced by a company in Indiana and sold by a store in Illinois. Because of the commerce clause, our government can, among other things, outlaw the use of poor materials at the company that makes the shoes, and protect workers who transport the shoes against unfair labor practices by their employer. Today, such things as transportation, telephone communication, TV and radio transmission, and labor-and-management relations are regulated under the authority of the commerce clause.

A second way the Constitution enters our daily lives is through a passage known as the "general welfare clause." The Preamble authorizes our government to "promote the general welfare" of the citizens it serves. In the 1930s under President Roosevelt's New Deal, this meant providing jobs for people who didn't have them, social insurance for the old, sick, and disabled, and public assistance for poor people. In our own time "general welfare" has come to include housing and transportation programs, environmental protection, funding for education and health, safety regulations in the workplace, and a host of other things. None of these things is mentioned in the Constitution, but none of them really has to be. The language of the Constitution flows into the spaces that we leave open for it. Our needs as a nation provide the opportunity. The Constitution simply adapts—and endures.

The Constitution in the Future

Many years ago, one of our chief justices remarked that "the Constitution is what the judges say it is." If this is true, and if judges' opinions are influenced by the society around them, then all of us are in some way involved in determining what the Constitution is and what it will be. Whether we are concerned or unconcerned, what we think will affect the way the Constitution operates in the future.

1919 — *Schenck v. United States*
Extended the right to freedom of speech.

1925 — *Dunbra v. United States*
Limited the right of government to search citizens and seize property.

Brown v. Board of Education of Topeka
Overturned *Plessy v. Ferguson* and said that segregation violated equal protection under the law.

1954

Gideon v. Wainwright
Declared that all accused persons have the right to a lawyer, even if they cannot afford to pay for one.

New York Times v. Sullivan
Affirmed the freedom of the press.

1963
1964

Miranda v. Arizona
Established certain basic rights of people accused of crimes.

1966

Of course, the Constitution can survive without us. It has done so in the past and, with luck, will continue to do so long after we are gone. But *how* it survives is a different matter. The Constitution is not quite a self-regulating engine. It needs occasional attention, and also a sense of purpose, to do the job it can. The Constitution makes an excellent guide, but it can only take us where we, the people, want to be led.

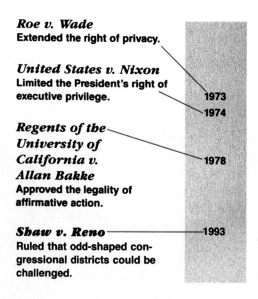

Roe v. Wade
Extended the right of privacy.

United States v. Nixon
Limited the President's right of executive privilege.

1973
1974

Regents of the University of California v. Allan Bakke
Approved the legality of affirmative action.

1978

Shaw v. Reno
Ruled that odd-shaped congressional districts could be challenged.

1993

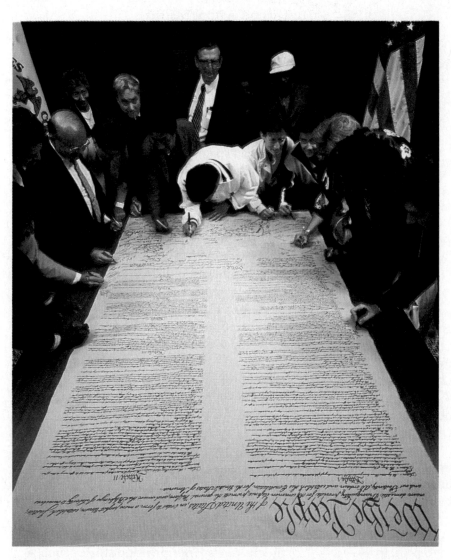

People confirm their faith in the Constitution by signing a copy of it. Our Constitution has endured two hundred years of social and political changes.

ADDITIONAL MATERIALS Use Worksheets 19 and 20 pages T40 and T41 in conjunction with this lesson. In preparation for the test on pages T42–T45 have students take the Constitution

67

Self Test on pages 15–18 and use the Review Outline on pages T20 and T21.

Case Study: The Hazelwood Case

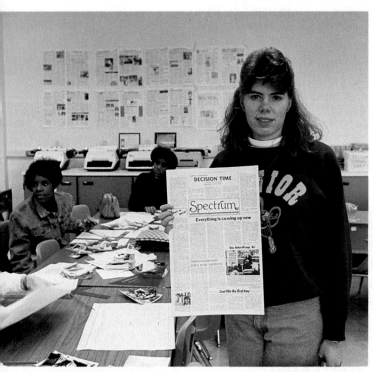

High school students in Hazelwood, Missouri, felt their free speech rights were violated when their principal removed stories from the school newspaper. The Supreme Court supported the principal's actions with its ruling.

Do First Amendment rights apply to students? How far can school officials go in limiting free speech in newspapers and other publications sponsored by the school? These were among the questions raised in a recent Supreme Court case involving the censorship of a student newspaper at a high school in Hazelwood, Missouri.

In the spring of 1983, the principal of Hazelwood East High School examined the pages of a student newspaper scheduled to be printed a few days later. The *Spectrum* was written and edited by students at the school, and reviewing it before publication was one of the principal's normal tasks. The principal was disturbed by

two of the stories. One involved three unnamed students who had become pregnant; the other was a report on problems facing students whose parents were divorced. The principal objected to what he considered violations of privacy. Since there was no time to rewrite the stories, he decided to pull them from the paper.

When the newspaper was published without the stories, three students on the paper's staff protested that their rights of speech and press had been violated. They filed suit against the Hazelwood School District.

Following one ruling against the students and another ruling for them, the case was brought before the Supreme Court. The Court ruled in favor of the school district and the principal.

The Supreme Court rejected the students' main argument. No rights had been violated by the principal's action, the majority verdict stated. The principal's concerns over privacy and the impact of the stories in question were enough reason to censor the paper. The principal was simply applying "community standards" in deciding what the students might publish, and had acted in a way consistent with established school policy.

The *Hazelwood* verdict was not unexpected. Other rulings had already shown that the Supreme Court would not grant students the same constitutional protections as adults. Still the decision came as a blow to supporters of students' rights—and to the idea that press rights ought to be protected wherever a press is found.

REVIEW

1. What arguments would you use to support the idea of students' rights to free expression?

2. What arguments would you use against a student newspaper printing stories such as those in the Hazelwood case?

Name _____

REVIEW 4
Lessons 8–10

A. VOCABULARY—AMENDMENTS 11–27

For each of the following quotations, fill in the missing word or phrase.
In the blank following each quotation, write in the number of the
amendment in which the quotation can be found.

1. "All persons born or _____naturalized_____ in the United States, and subject to the jurisdiction thereof, are citizens of the United States. . . ." Amendment ____14____

2. "The right of the citizens of the United States to vote shall not be denied or _____abridged_____ . . . on account of sex." Amendment ____22____

3. "The Congress shall have power to lay and collect taxes on incomes, from whatever source derived, without _____apportionment_____ among the several states. . . ." Amendment ____16____

4. "Whenever the President transmits to the _____president pro tempore_____ of the Senate and the speaker of the House his written declaration that he is unable to discharge the powers and duties of his office. . . ." Amendment ____25____

5. "The eighteenth article of amendment of the Constitution of the United States is hereby _____repealed_____." Amendment ____21____

6. "Neither slavery nor _____involuntary servitude_____, except as a punishment for crime . . . shall exist within the United States. . . ." Amendment ____13____

7. "The manufacture, sale, or transportation of _____intoxicating liquors_____ within . . . the United States . . . is hereby prohibited." Amendment ____18____

8. "The right of citizens of the United States to vote in any . . . election for President . . . shall not be denied or abridged . . . by reason of failure to pay any _____poll tax_____ or other tax." Amendment ____24____

B. CRITICAL THINKING

1. What are some reasons why being able to amend the Constitution is important for the continued success of our government?

Answers will vary. Possible responses: The Constitution must be able

to adjust to changing conditions in order to work; if people couldn't

change the Constitution, a new one would have to be written if

something needed to be changed.

_____

_____

2. Choose *one* of the following proposed amendments to the Constitution: The Equal Rights Amendment, The School Prayer Amendment, or The Right to Life Amendment. Tell what the amendment is intended to change and explain why you favor or oppose the proposed amendment.

Answers will vary. Student answers should include a general idea of

what the amendment proposes and give one or more reasons for

supporting or opposing the amendment.

_____

_____

C. FACTS AND IDEAS

Match each of the following amendment summaries with the number of the amendment to which it applies.

<u>23</u> 1. Residents of the District of Columbia enjoy the right to vote in presidential elections.

<u>15</u> 2. No citizen may be deprived of the right to vote on account of race or color.

<u>18</u> 3. The manufacture, sale, and transportation of alcohol is forbidden throughout the United States.

<u>25</u> 4. In the event of a President's disability, the Vice-President becomes Acting President.

<u>19</u> 5. Women acquire the right to vote in all elections at all levels of government.

<u>11</u> 6. No state can be sued by a citizen of another state.

<u>14</u> 7. No person can be denied the rights guaranteed by the Constitution without due process of the law.

<u>24</u> 8. Poll taxes cannot be used to restrict the rights of voters.

<u>26</u> 9. All citizens have the right to vote when they reach the age of eighteen years.

<u>27</u> 10. Congressional salaries are restricted.

Amendment 11
Amendment 14
Amendment 15
Amendment 18
Amendment 19
Amendment 23
Amendment 24
Amendment 25
Amendment 26
Amendment 27

★ ★ CONSTITUTION SELF TEST ★ ★

Circle the letter of the response that best answers each question or completes each statement.

1. When was the Constitution officially ratified?
   a. July 4, 1776
   c. January 24, 1791
   b. March 4, 1789
   d. May 1, 1803

2. How many states were needed before the Constitution could take effect?
   a. all thirteen
   b. a simple majority
   c. nine of the thirteen
   d. at least three of the largest

3. What is the *main* idea of the Preamble?
   a. to state the purpose of the Constitution
   b. to set limits on the authority of the federal government
   c. to establish the relationship of the branches of government
   d. to explain the reasoning behind the break with England

4. Which of the following is NOT one of the branches of government?
   a. judicial
   c. legislative
   b. executive
   d. military

5. Which of the following belongs to Congress? (There is more than one correct answer.)
   a. Supreme Court
   b. House of Representatives
   c. Senate
   d. President

6. How is the membership of the House of Representatives determined?
   a. by the apportioned population of the states
   b. by two representatives from each state
   c. by the governors of states according to a formula established by Congress
   d. by the legislature of each state

7. Which of the following is NOT necessary to be elected to the House of Representatives?
   a. be a citizen of the United States
   b. be at least thirty-five years old
   c. live in the state he or she represents
   d. live in the United States at least seven years

8. How long is the term of office for a representative?
   a. two years
   c. six years
   b. four years
   d. for life

9. The officer who presides over the House of Representatives is called the _____.
   a. President
   c. speaker
   b. president pro tempore
   d. chairman

10. How is representation in the Senate determined?
    a. by the apportioned population of the states
    b. by two representatives from each state
    c. by the state governors according to a formula established by Congress
    d. by number determined by the legislature of each state

11. Which of the following are qualifications needed to be a senator? (There is more than one correct answer.)
    a. must be at least thirty years of age
    b. must have been a citizen for at least nine years
    c. must live in the state he or she represents
    d. must have previously served in the House of Representatives

12. How long is the term of office for a senator?
    a. two years
    c. six years
    b. four years
    d. for life

13. The officer who presides over the Senate when the Vice-President in not in attendance is called the _____.

a. President

b. president pro tempore

c. speaker

d. chairman

14. The _____ has the sole power to impeach.

a. Senate

b. Supreme Court

c. House of Representatives

d. electoral college

15. After an officeholder is impeached, the _____ has the sole power to try the case.

a. Senate

b. Supreme Court

c. House of Representatives

d. electoral college

16. The debates, laws, and other information about what goes on in the legislative branch is reported in _____.

a. the local newspaper

b. *The Legislative Forum*

c. the docket of the Supreme Court

d. *The Congressional Record*

17. The Constitution says that the Congress must meet _____.

a. at least once every two years

b. at least once each year

c. for a total of six months, every other year

d. only whenever they have legislation waiting to become law

18. A bill may be proposed by _____. (There is more than one correct answer.)

a. A member of the House of Representatives

b. A member of the Senate

c. The President or Vice-President

d. A justice of the Supreme Court

19. The executive branch's power to refuse to sign a bill into law is called _____.

a. right of refusal

b. legislative bargaining

c. presidential review

d. presidential veto

20. If both houses of Congress wish to have a bill become law, but each has changed the original, the bill must go to _____.

a. the President

b. a conference committee

c. the Supreme Court

d. the sub-committee where it originated

21. All of the following are *expressed powers* of the Congress except the power _____.

a. to tax   c. to coin money

b. to borrow money   d. to declare laws unconstitutional

22. Another term for "implied powers" is _____.

a. elastic   c. absolute

b. expressed   d. stated

23. What powers are forbidden to Congress? (There is more than one correct answer.)

a. to make writs of habeas corpus

b. to grant titles of nobility

c. to pass ex post facto laws

d. to make bills of attainder

24. Article II deals with _____.

a. the executive branch

b. the judicial branch

c. the legislative branch

d. the rights of an individual

25. The executive branch is made up of _____. (There is more than one correct answer.)

a. President

b. Vice-President

c. chief justice

d. cabinet officers

26. The main job of the President is _____.

    a. to enforce the laws of the United States

    b. to interpret the Constitution

    c. to initiate legislation

    d. to direct the actions of the standing congressional committees

27. The President is elected by _____.

    a. the electoral college

    b. a direct vote of the citizens

    c. the legislatures of the various states

    d. the majority of the House of Representatives and Senate

28. How long is the term of the President and Vice-President?

    a. two years

    b. four years

    c. six years

    d. eight years

29. If the President is unable to serve, the Vice-President takes his place. After the Vice-President, the next federal official in line for the presidency is _____.

    a. the secretary of state

    b. the secretary of defense

    c. the president pro tempore of the Senate

    d. the speaker of the House of Representatives

30. All of the following are powers of the President EXCEPT _____.

    a. declaring war

    b. granting reprieves and pardons

    c. executing the laws

    d. presenting a state of the Union address each year

31. Who of the following is a member of the President's cabinet?

    a. speaker of the House

    b. Chief Justice of the Supreme Court

    c. president pro tempore of the Senate

    d. secretary of state

32. How are cabinet officers chosen?

    a. by the President alone

    b. by the President, with consent of the House

    c. by the President, with consent of the Senate

    d. by the President, with consent of the chief justice

33. Article III deals with _____.

    a. the executive branch

    b. the judicial branch

    c. the legislative branch

    d. the rights of an individual

34. How many justices—including the chief justice—are on the Supreme Court?

    a. five

    b. seven

    c. nine

    d. eleven

35. How long does a justice of the Supreme Court remain a member of the Court?

    a. two years

    b. four years

    c. six years

    d. for life

36. What *two* things could happen for someone accused of treason to be convicted?

    a. Two witnesses to the treason must testify against the person.

    b. The Supreme Court must declare the person guilty.

    c. The Congress must impeach and convict the person.

    d. The accused person could confess to the act of treason.

37. New states can be admitted to the union only with the permission of _____.

    a. the President   c. the Supreme Court

    b. the Congress   d. two-thirds approval of the state legislatures

38. How can an amendment to the Constitution be proposed? (There is more than one correct answer.)

    a. by the President, with majority approval of the cabinet

    b. by a two-thirds vote of both houses of Congress

    c. by a convention called by two-thirds of the states

    d. by the agreement of a majority of the justices of the Supreme Court

39. How many amendments make up the Bill of Rights?

    a. the first six   c. the first ten

    b. 1–5 and 9–12   d. the first eight, plus 13 and 21

40. Which amendment guarantees freedom of religion, speech, press, assembly, and petition?

    a. first   c. ninth

    b. fifth   d. none of these

41. Quartering troops is restricted in the Constitution. Quartering troops means _____.

    a. putting forts or arsenals in only 25 percent of the states

    b. placing soldiers on the public lands of the states

    c. placing soldiers in private homes

    d. housing soldiers in areas where civilians may otherwise meet

42. A court order allowing an individual or his property to be searched or seized is called a _____.

    a. treaty of understanding   c. executive privilege

    b. warrant   d. writ of habeas corpus

43. Any powers *not* specifically denied to the states or given to Congress are called _____.

    a. limited   c. reserved

    b. implied   d. assured

Matching   Write the letter of the amendment in the blank next to the statement that best represents the amendment.

_____ 44. right to bear arms

_____ 45. rights of citizens

_____ 46. eighteen-year-old vote

_____ 47. freedom of speech

_____ 48. abolition of slavery

_____ 49. right of women to vote

_____ 50. income tax

_____ 51. quartering of troops

_____ 52. bail and punishment

_____ 53. suits against states

_____ 54. abolition of poll tax

_____ 55. search and seizure

_____ 56. speedy and fair trial

_____ 57. civil suits

_____ 58. repeal of prohibition

_____ 59. rights of an accused person

_____ 60. election of the President and Vice-President

_____ 61. limit on presidential terms

_____ 62. presidential disability and succession

_____ 63. powers reserved to the states

_____ 64. prohibition of alcoholic beverages

_____ 65. "lame duck" amendment

_____ 66. direct election of senators

_____ 67. powers reserved to the people

_____ 68. right of Washington, D.C., to vote in presidential elections

_____ 69. restraint of congressional salaries

a. Amendment 1
b. Amendment 2
c. Amendment 3
d. Amendment 4
e. Amendment 5
f. Amendment 6
g. Amendment 7
h. Amendment 8
i. Amendment 9
j. Amendment 10
k. Amendment 11
l. Amendment 12
m. Amendment 13
n. Amendment 14
o. Amendment 15
p. Amendment 16
q. Amendment 17
r. Amendment 18
s. Amendment 19
t. Amendment 20
u. Amendment 21
v. Amendment 22
w. Amendment 23
x. Amendment 24
y. Amendment 25
z. Amendment 26
aa. Amendment 27